# BUSINESS GAMES

MARTIN G. GRODER, M.D., is a psychiatrist and business consultant, and one of America's foremost practitioners of management psychiatry. A graduate of Columbia College and Columbia University's College of Physicians and Surgeons, Dr. Groder served for three years as Warden of the Federal Center for Correctional Research in Marion, Illinois.

Dr. Groder is a member of the American Psychiatric Association, and is also a Special Field Teaching Member of the International Transactional Analysis Association. He has written several papers and articles for medical journals.

JOHN VON HARTZ, a free-lance writer and playwright, has written for major book publishers and periodicals. He received a 1981–82 Guggenheim Fellowship for playwriting.

# BUSINESS GAMES

## HOW TO RECOGNIZE THE PLAYERS AND DEAL WITH THEM

MARTIN G. GRODER, M.D.

and

JOHN VON HARTZ

BOARDROOM® BOOKS

500 Fifth Avenue, New York, New York 10110

$50

Fifth Printing

Boardroom Books publishes the advice of
expert authorities in many fields. But the
use of a book is not a substitute for legal,
accounting, or other professional services.
Consult a competent professional for
answers to your specific questions.

Library of Congress Cataloging in Publication Data

Groder, Martin G.
   Business games; how to recognize the players and deal with them

   1. Personnel management   2. Psychology, Industrial.
1. Von Hartz, John, joint author.   II. Title
HF5549.G73        658.3'001'9        80-19095
ISBN 0-932648-14-2

Printed in the United States of America

# Table of Contents


Introduction.......................................................1

Part I:    Optimistic Risk Games ....................................10

  1.      Workaholic .................................................11

  2.      Crocodile ..................................................17

  3.      Making a Score .............................................25

  4.      Taking .....................................................34

  5.      Sexual Harassment .........................................41

  6.      Cowboy .....................................................46

  7.      Have I Got a Deal for You ..................................52

  8.      Sweathog ...................................................59

  9.      Emperor ....................................................64

10.      Territory ..................................................72

11.      Office Marriage ............................................80

12.      Raw Power ..................................................87

Part II:   Pessimistic Risk Games ......................................92

13.        Are You Out to Get Me? ....................................93

14.        Arson .....................................................102

15.        Snooper ...................................................108

16.        Work the Man ..............................................115


Part III:  Optimistic Security Games ..................................120

17.        Give Away .................................................121

18.        True Believer .............................................130

19.        Goody Two-Shoes ...........................................137

20.        Father Knows Best .........................................143

21.        Daddy Will Provide ........................................149


Part IV:   Pessimistic Security Games .................................159

22.        Sacred Cow ................................................160

23.        Hell, I'm Only Human ......................................168

24.        Only I Know Where It Is ...................................173

25.        But at Least ..............................................183

26.        Hanging On ................................................190

27.        Good Old Sam ..............................................196

28.        Bitter--But Loyal .........................................200

29.        Cover Your Tracks .........................................206

30.        You're Holding Me Back ....................................215

31.        Overload ..................................................221

Part V:   Workaday Games ...............................227

          Chronic Lateness .......................228

          Procrastination .......................230

          Compulsive Fast Finisher ..............231

          Double Standard .......................232

          Slave Driver ..........................233

          Compression Freak .....................235

          Petty Capitalist ......................237

          Just Barely Making It .................238

          Absent on Monday ......................240

          Oddly Out of Uniform ..................242

          Surly and Uncooperative ...............246

          Office Romeo/Office Tease .............248

          Self-Righteous ........................250

          Chronic Complainer ....................251

          Babbling ..............................253

          Humble Mumble .........................255

          Distracter ............................256

          Bluster (and Yelp) ....................257

          Bully in the Chair ....................257

          Psychological Hypochrondriacs .........258

# INTRODUCTION

Sooner or later, every businessman finds himself confronted by problems in his operation that defy solution. These difficulties may seem at first glance to be technical--shrinking profits, low sales, and the like. Yet the appropriate technical solutions--cutting costs, adding salesmen, and so on--don't work. In fact, the solutions often make the problem more severe. They disturb the daily functioning of the business, jar the morale of the staff, and even threaten the physical and mental health of the manager.

Baffled and confused, the manager sees himself trapped by forces he thinks he can't control. In this state of crisis, rational managers may contemplate the irrational--abandoning their beloved businesses or professions. They yearn for new lifestyles where the challenges are more modest and malleable.

## Psychological roots of the problems

The plain fact: These beleagured managers are victims of problems that are understandable, and, with the correct procedures, capable of solution. The difficulties can even be summed up in the unthreatening word "games"; they only appear insurmountable because the manager is blind to their root causes, which are the psychological quirks of his personnel-- and himself. Remember: People live in a world they create. Problems caused by people can be cured by people. The games played by employees must be faced.  To ignore them, or wish them away, is to risk heavy psychological and financial costs.


## Game playing

My teacher and mentor, Dr. Eric Berne, first popularized the game concept with his landmark book Games People Play. To Dr. Berne, people with psychological aberrations were acting out roles--playing games--without being totally aware of their actions. These games were adopted through life experiences--that is, they were learned. Usually, the games worked against the better nature of the players and cast them in a negative light. Alcoholism, sexual games, underworld games, and other antisocial games were all considered acquired behavior.

Since these games are learned, however, they can also be unlearned. Thus the games players can often be taught to abandon their games--and to become truly productive members of the work force. The underlying concept of this book is to show managers and employees the nature of the games that are played in business today and to suggest ways and means for dealing with them.

2

## Meeting basic needs

Why do people play these games? All of us have basic human needs. Meeting these needs often generates emotional conflict--adventure vs. security, intimacy vs. independence, excitement vs. conformity. When a person cannot reconcile these clashing priorities, he may choose to play a game based on his distorted perception of them.

Some of these distortions are culturally supported, such as those for the Workaholic (page 11). The American culture admires the person who gives himself to his work--and adulates the way he drives himself to achieve his business goals, even though he usually wrecks his physical health, loses friendships, and may alienate his family. Despite these deficits, he is still hailed as a "success." The game of COWBOY demonstrates an American love affair with the isolated individualist who does what he wants, when he wants, then rides off into the sunset. Although the game meets the needs of achievement and excitement, it avoids serious commitment. Yet it appears "good" because the culture approves it.

## A web of games

A word about the games themselves. Do not leap to simplistic conclusions about them. Spotting and rooting out one game is difficult enough, but most players are involved simultaneously in many. The inventive human mind, once skewed, spins a spider's web of games--often with the unwitting cooperation of other players who supply complementary twists. Sometimes a player is entwined in a tangle of games, each tied to others.

Some games have such pathological symptoms and lead to such inhuman actions that the player must be driven from the business before he destroys it. Those playing the vicious game called ARE YOU OUT TO GET ME, for example, should be treated with the deference afforded a cornered, starving tiger. Most games, however, are psychological aberrations that can be cured with the proper approaches.

But because we are trying to make matters as clear as possible, in discussing the games there will be times when we make this intricate subject sound rather simple. This direct approach is only for the sake of understanding the problem and learning what to do about it.

## Organizing the work

The games in this book have been organized according to the intersection of opposed personal attitudes of considered importance to the success of a business--optimism and pessimism, willingness to take risks and interest in security. These attitudes are chosen arbitrarily by the player as a means of dealing with the world and its risks. Usually, the player brings them to the job with him every day. But sometimes, the work itself helps him form his attitude about his job and himself.

Optimism and pessimism are the crucial issues. The optimist observes the complexity of human actions in its most favorable light--and visualizes how each action will meet desired needs. The pessimist regards the same complexity as a source of possible failure--or at least of difficulties--and as a reason for hesitation and withdrawal. In optimistic games, the player pushes for more of what he feels he can hope for. In pessimistic games, the player strives constantly to avoid the feared negative outcome.

The largest portion of the book deals with the more complex psycho-

4

logical games. But often the employee behavior problem is a small, annoying one, an irritating trait in an otherwise productive person. These are discussed in the section titled Workaday Games.

## Answering basic questions

In addressing the games, particularly the more complex ones, I try to answer such questions as these: How does the game originate in the player? What are some of its psychological and sociological roots? What are the costs to your company? What are the telltale signs of the game? How does a player manage to be hired in the first place? What job is he suited for? Whom does he get along with? What can be done to correct the game? And what positive aspects can be drawn from the experience?

## Simple language

I have attempted throughout the book to shy away from fancy terms. Familiar speech takes precedence over invented language. While useful at times, an invented vocabulary can, through improper translation, sacrifice accuracy. Dr. Berne taught, and I believe, that Latin and Greek medical terms do not convey the truth. Only through intuitive illumination followed by reason will a manager perceive the people-problems that plague his business. Plain English is the language of the problems and also of the solutions.

On the subject of language, just a note about the use of the third-person singular pronoun. I have chosen the pronoun "he" for a player, even for games indulged in by both men and women. It is a measure of convenience, not an implication of sexual superiority--or inferiority. Only when women are indisputably the players or their victims do I employ the pronoun "she."

## Special terms

During the course of the book, I will occasionally mention such terms as "Human Potential Movement" and "OKness," which need brief definition. The Human Potential Movement (HPM) is a loosely allied collection of organizations, theories, and practices developed since the early 1960s. Humanism is its philosophical rooting. Heavy emphasis is placed on individual freedom, expansion of human awareness, development of the individual's potential, encouragement of increased creativity, personal happiness, and openness of communication and emotionality. Often the movement calls for an almost cultlike adherence to certain forms, practices, and dictums.

Most of the self-help books that flood today's literary marketplace are expressions of the Human Potential Movement. The HPM is also represented by classes, groups, retreats, outings, and study courses at service organizations such as the "Y." Some groups combine their study centers with a specialized lifestyle; the most famous of these is Esalen.

The term "OKness" is a basic assumption of Transactional Analysis, the discipline founded by Dr. Berne. Transactional Analysis (TA) states that an individual's self-opinion is crucial to his well-being and ability to be productive. OKness is the feeling that accompanies a positive self-opinion. It is my fervent belief, as taught by TA, that every person is born with this positive self-opinion. All negative self-opinion is learned in the process of growing up. Since this negativity is learned, it can be unlearned.

My unshakable stance is that people are OK. If they are playing games,
it is because they have learned to do so for a variety of intricate reasons
and motivations. Once they see the nature of their games, they are on their
way toward conquering them and achieving a feeling of "OKness."


## Therapist and consultant

Other terms used in the book may benefit from review here. I will often
refer to either a psychotherapist or a consultant. A psychotherapist is a
professional who offers a relationship, a particular theory and practice
that places the person and his problem in a framework. In doing this, the
psychotherapist defines the possible courses of action that can end or
alleviate the problem. During the course of this problem solving, the
therapist often provides independent support and encouragement to the
player.

While the therapist works with an individual, a couple, or a family,
the consultant's relationship is with a business or organization. Many
business consultants are not psychotherapists, but their mode of operation is similar. A business consultant usually has a more organized for-
mat; a psychotherapist is more open-ended in his approach.

Naturally, there are differences in the technologies, theories, and
professional backgrounds between a psychotherapist and a consultant, but
there are professionals who do both. I am one of those who found a sympathetic union between the two. In fact, it has been my experience that consultation is nothing less than a marriage between therapeutic and business
skills.

## The useful work contract

In the course of our explorations, I shall refer often, particularly when discussing solutions, to a work contract between the manager and the game player. These work contracts are almost always verbal. They provide a two-way, adult method of reaching agreement and resolution between the people who have been involved in the problematic behavior that we call games. The work contract is an important tool to resolving games because of the logic and clarity it brings. Games flourish in obfuscation, vagueness, misunderstandings, and double-talk. The work contract helps to eliminate these conditions and clears the air.

Here's the anatomy of a work contract:

First, there must be two-way communication in which both parties agree that they agree on what the problem is. They must also agree that they will find a solution together. Two-way communication means that the employer does not impose a solution on an unwitting player.

Next there should be an agreement about terms, the nature of the solutions, and the time frame in which the solutions will be given a chance to work. This includes acknowledgement that there will be periodic evaluations to see how the solution is progressing--or if the problem is recurring.

There must also be a sense of what will happen if the solutions do not hold up; the outcome can range all the way from a change of assignment to dismissal. The contract is set when there is mutual consent to the terms and to the competence of the engaging parties to proceed with the solution. The terms must be legal and all parties involved must receive valid consideration for performance.

## Problems into opportunities

From my experience in working with people interested in helping themselves and others, I offer a few final words. There is no magic in this or any other self-help book. There is guidance and direction about ways to focus your energy toward transforming problems into opportunities.

The basic principle that I hold, along with my colleagues in Transactional Analysis, is that people own their own lives. You are free to alter any part of your behavior that is within your human capacity.

Remember: The positive events in life have come primarily from the good choices, judgments, and implementations you have made--with perhaps a bit of luck thrown in. Conversely, the unpalatable events have resulted from bad choices, judgments, and implementations, which were often based on ignorance about how to meet basic human needs.

The games described are not diseases. They are patterns of observable behavior associated with feelings, attitudes, and ideas. Some require concentrated professional help to cure; a few dwell beyond the reach of even the most modern techniques. But the most common games should be seen as resulting from a series of choices made by the player. Once this is understood, the pathway to solution begins to open.

Good luck.

Martin G. Groder, M.D.

Part One

# OPTIMISTIC RISK GAMES

The players of these games are risk-takers who are not afraid to push themselves forward. OPTIMISTIC RISK games are played by those who are confident of winning. The attitude of the players reflects some of those found in the most successful businessmen, among them an avowed willingness to take chances to achieve goals.

Chapter One

# WORKAHOLIC

Just as alcoholism is one of America's principal mental ailments, the WORKAHOLIC game is among its chief social disorders. The precept is simple --hard work is the answer to every question, the solution to every problem, and the only reliable route to success.

Belief in this precept breeds a singleness of purpose that makes the Workaholic an object of admirationa in the American culture--and indeed, the game embodies some highly admirable traits (e.g., persistence, thoroughness, dedication). In any case, it gives the player such satisfaction that he gradually abandons other areas of his life--family, friends, recreation, hobbies, community activities.

## Good people work hard

In fact, most players excuse this game by hiding behind the American

Work Ethic. From childhood we are told that people who work hard are not only good, they are rewarded--with a lot of money. The next logical link in this chain of reasoning: the more you work, the richer you become, the better person you are. This conviction has driven and supported most of the country's great entrepreneurs, businessmen, and financiers.

Though the Workaholic is lionized as a symbol of achievement, those close to him, both family and business associates, are squashed by the pressure he creates in his zeal for the job.

## Some pull it off

Part of the attractive mystique of this game is that a few of the best players manage to pull it off. Sometimes it is a legendary business figure, such as Andrew Carnegie, sometimes the hard-driving, up-to-date chief of an international conglomerate. In any case, a few in every generation stand as successful symbols of the game--and live to a ripe old age to enjoy the fruits of their labor. But the vast majority of Workaholics are not so lucky. Though well motivated, and even dedicated, they are traveling down an increasingly rocky road that will dead-end in sorrow.

## Mapping the game

The game is easy to chart. In its early phases, the player makes an extraordinary effort to earn a name and build a reputation. He pushes himself mercilessly to master the skills of business not taught in school. This intensive apprenticeship generally brings success and earns the respect of his superiors. Thus rewarded, the player is encouraged, in effect, to neglect growth in all other areas of his life. He is left with the notion that work is truly the only rewarding activity--everything else is a waste of time. And the more the player works, the greater his tangible gains--salary, promotions, and a growing reputation as an achiever. Under the influence of this universal recognition, he increasingly denies all other areas of his life.

Sooner or later the problems surface. It may take years, but eventually, signs appear: the body fails from lack of attention, the wife leaves and the family breaks up, personal friends abandon him as he abandons them (he has little time for the social niceties--let alone for unadorned companionship). Instead of facing up to these real problems, the Workaholic throws himself deeper into his job. Just as the alcoholic seeks to find a solution to his drinking problem through more booze, the Workaholic chooses to work himself out of his difficulties with more work. In the terminal stage, the Workaholic is left with nothing but his work and his professional peers as friends. He stays doggedly on the job, hoping only to die with his boots on.

## Proven pathology

With all the cultural forces working to support it, it is no wonder that only recently has this dismal pattern been recognized and labeled as pathological. It is extremely difficult to reveal an article of faith as a destructive game. But medical evidence now conclusively links excessive work, especially when accompanied by physical inactivity, to such common and serious ailments as cardiac disease and ulcers. Workaholism has also been revealed as harmful in psychiatric studies that connect it with mental disorders.

There are increasing signs of cultural support for not following the pattern. But the signs are still random and infrequent, and more is made of them than they deserve. Like the hard-drinking churchgoer who avows temperance every Sunday morning, most Workaholics continue on their path, paying lip service to concern about their health while continuing the long, grueling work days.

## Women as Workaholics

The culture also forces many women into the game, especially those who wish to rise in the executive ranks. It says, in effect, you must give your life to your work if you wish to succeed in the male-dominated business world. Otherwise, you can stay back and do less demanding work. Or, you can give up, marry, and raise a family. It is a general rule that women who have ascended highest in business have had to adopt the game.

## Incalculable costs

At first, the game seems cost-free. In the early and middle phases, the player works day and night endowing the company with his energy, ideas, and total involvement. Thus, the game is all benefits for the organization. In the later phases, however, the game is all costs. By then the player is usually in his 40's or 50's, a time when he should be at his professional peak. Instead, he starts to suffer the physical and social deprivations brought on by years of overeffort. This is when key executives may suddenly die, suffer physical breakdowns, experience deep depressions, go through bitter divorces. At work, there may be a tendency to use poor judgment--even periods of inability to function. The costs to both the player and the company are incalculable.

## Signs of a player

What actions indicate that an employee is a practicing or potential Workaholic? The player never leaves at quitting time, even if he has no compelling reason to stay. He hangs on to do a little extra work or to help someone else who is behind schedule. He may even stick around just to talk to his colleagues about work. No job is too small to dissuade a Workaholic from staying until it is completed, even though doing it may interfere with his family--or other valid personal concern.

## Finding the cures

Because most bosses feed this game with praise and money, they are part of the problem--and the solution. They must be sure that company policies do not accelerate the Workaholic pattern. An executive's family and community responsibilities must be allowed space--for the sake of long-term effectiveness in the job. At times the player should be barred from his job for his own good--warned, for instance, that continued night and weekend work will only lead to his dissolution, despite the short-term gain for the company.

For his part, the Workaholic must learn to establish priorities along with work early in his career. If he is trying to avoid a marital problem, he should be encouraged to work with the marriage rather than run away by staying late at the office.

Nor does dealing with a personal problem mean devoting all off-duty time to it. The quality of the time spent is as important as its duration. A

family outing will do more to reunite its members, for example, than long
hours in front of the TV together, or an evening spent at home out of a grudg-
ing sense of obligation. These are exercises in which everyone ends up
feeling deprived.

If any of your employees--or you--are locked in the WORKAHOLIC game,
the only way out may be through professional consultation. This is particularly true when the game makes everything go wrong, even the work setting. When the problems of the Workaholic finally prevent him from working, his innermost defense is gone.

## Keeping control for success

Is the game all bad? The Workaholic makes the wheels of business turn
smoother and faster--until he breaks down. The player must search his soul
--perhaps with help from you, his boss--to answer these questions: Is work
all I want from life? Is money all I desire? Do I realize that I'm probably
headed for a major crisis?

Like social drinking, the cultural support pattern of working hard
and achieving success is acceptable as long as the person doesn't allow
himself to place little--or no--importance in living the rest of his life.
By keeping hard work within reasonable bounds, the success pattern can be
followed without slipping into the game.

# Chapter Two

# CROCODILE

A Crocodile loves the taste of human flesh. He enjoys firing people. He likes making workers squirm by warning them to tighten up their performance or face elimination. A Crocodile is useful at a time of business housecleaning, but his appetite is insatiable; he will find victims long after all necessary cuts in personnel are made.

Be careful: This is a tough game. A Crocodile could eat your job and devour your company.

## A taste of blood

A Crocodile is out front about his feelings--he looks, talks, and acts like the meanest SOB in the river. He expounds the philosophy of dog-eat-dog and derides weakness or tenderness in anyone else. He will claim to be productive--and some Crocodiles are--but his real joy is in destroying

competition and wrecking the plans of advancement of his fellow employees.
He has few kind words for anyone, and welcomes the thought of cleaning
house: "If the SOB's aren't doing the job, of course I'll get rid of them."

In sophisticated circles, the Crocodile can be subtle and diplo-
matic. He may be identified, however, by the trail of blood he leaves behind. This trail is to be found in his references; evaluate them carefully.
Try to find a near-victim at his previous place of employment, someone who
still bears the scars from his teethmarks--his immediate superior or a
competing colleague.

Ask this former fellow worker such questions as: "If he had problems,
in what area might they occur?" Be alert to veiled answers like this: "Well,
he was kind of coldblooded. He didn't have a lot of feeling for other people. He was a little abrasive. Some people couldn't work with him. Those
people are no longer here."

Even a worker who was nearly done in by a Crocodile isn't anxious to
tell tales on him. Still, don't be afraid to persist in asking questions
about the suspected Crocodile's attitudes toward people. The worst mistake you can make is in fooling yourself into believing a future employee
isn't a Crocodile when he really is. For your own safety, you must identify
a player right from the start.

## Demotion and exile

Most Crocodiles are found in middle and top management jobs, because
the true player must have responsibility for human lives. A Crocodile is a
hard-nosed, tough-minded, competitive manager. In a committee evaluating
personnel, the player is quick to recommend harsh punishments such as job

demotion, exile to a remote branch, and even firing for minor shortcomings. He tends to ridicule humanitarian company policies or generosity toward fellow employees.

When he is involved in office politics, a Crocodile reveals himself by providing the boss with damaging information.

Example: A manager who was having an affair with his secretary was also a rival to the Crocodile. The Crocodile was the first one to bring the intrigue to the boss's attention. He supplied details: "I guess you thought Jones was working on the new account. Be he spends most of his time behind his closed door making love to his secretary."

In this way he tried to put the boss in a Crocodile position. Crocodiles enjoy spectator sports. If he can turn you, the boss, into a Crocodile, he will gleefully watch the flesh being torn. It's almost as good to him as doing the eating himself, especially since you, the boss, are taking the responsibility. But your own personal security is threatened by the Crocodile, since he often finds the flesh of the boss himself most tasty.

## Handy in a crisis

A Crocodile is best hired in time of crisis. That is when his hard, aggressive nature is required as the business battles for survival. In combat, the Crocodile is a very vigorous, successful warrior who usually proves his worth.

Example: A space-age products development subsidiary in business for five years had never turned a profit--in fact, its losses totalled $7 million. It had 167 employees, many of whom were outright losers--misfits from the parent corporation who were dumped into the subsidiary. When a new manager took over the subsidiary, he hired a Crocodile as a general plant manager.

The Crocodile proved to have good technical abilities as well as a knack for getting rid of unwanted workers. The payroll soon fell from 167 to 82 employees, nor were the final 82 culled from the original 167. The Crocodile fired more than three-quarters of the original staff, then surrounded himself with 82 good workers. But the subsidiary was more productive and soon showed a profit.

The Crocodile also earns his keep during a recession when the boss is reluctant to make the cuts--jobs, salaries, perquisites--needed to keep the company afloat. While the top manager may not like to hurt his employees, many of whom are his friends, the Crocodile isn't upset at that prospect. He'll bear the brunt of the hatred and animosity such tough measures inspire.

## Keeping him where you can see him

Don't go on vacation and leave a Crocodile in charge. He may eat your chair and your desk.

Don't give him short-term, unsupervised powers. He is excellent at turning a temporary opportunity into a coup d'etat.

Another bad mistake is to have a Crocodile as a liaison between you and the people who hired you. A Crocodile should not be allowed to get close to anyone in a position to fire you as boss. Keep him in a subordinate position, blocked from direct personal contact with power sources.

Example: The manager of a booming subsidiary had a Crocodile as first deputy. The boss didn't like to make those mandatory trips to the central

20

office for meetings and planning sessions. He preferred to stay at the plant where the action was. Knowing the man in charge didn't like the trips, the Crocodile talked the boss into letting him go instead. After a few trips to the central office, the Crocodile had the top job as well as the nice corner office.

## Respect for force, contempt for weakness

Crocodiles swim well together. Since they fear each others' teeth, they rarely bite one another, at least openly.

They show respect for superior force. Thus, they get along well with subordinates, peers, and superiors who are at least as tough as they are.

They also get along with unassuming but highly productive people who are respected for their accomplishments. Good workers who don't push--or threaten--are acceptable to Crocodiles, but they are lethal with people who threaten them ineffectually. They have contempt for the weak, liberals, and humanitarians. Since compassion is deemed a sign of weakness, those who display any are discounted by a Crocodile.

## Matching force with force

Crocodiles don't make good pets. Use them only when necessary or not at all.

Never hire a Crocodile unless you can handle him by being as tough as he is. The only way to win the respect of a Crocodile is through superior power and finesse. Be relentless with him--any opening or hint of vulnerability will be exploited.

Even if you feel a match for the Crocodile, hire him only temporarily.

A Crocodile doesn't make a good permanent employee; there is no peace as long as he is part of the of the organization. Once he has served his purpose in the battle for the company's survival, he must be sent away or on to new wars within the organization.

Getting rid of a Crocodile sometimes requires finesse:

The boss of a small corporation had a favorite employee with whom he was playing DADDY WILL PROVIDE FOR THE LITTLE FELLA (pages 149-158). The boss wanted to fire the Little Fella but didn't have the heart to do it. He hired a Crocodile to fire the favorite. The Crocodile, however, was more interested in his own version of the game than he was in the boss's purpose: He flattered, seduced, and cajoled the Little Fella into associating with him against the boss. Sensing the conspiracy, the boss offered the Crocodile and the Little Fella a chance to buy a piece of the business. He sold them a losing branch that had been retarding the corporation's development--and moved both the Crocodile and the Little Fella off his payroll.

## Sounding alarms—and warnings

Since Crocodiles are hired only in times of company crisis--retrenchment, recession, fiscal setbacks--your employees and business associates must be kept informed when conditions are serious enough to mandate the hiring of a Crocodile.

There must be a general awareness throughout the firm that the business is deep in a genuine crisis. A warning should sound loudly and clearly that future decisions will be based on the survival of the organization.

Announce to all that the Crocodile is arriving. No one is immune from his hungry eye.

## Crocodiles in Command

Most bosses who are Crocodiles don't know they are. Firing unproductive people is part of being in command. So is being a bold leader who is unafraid of stepping on toes.

The boss might sense he's a Crocodile if he has a feeling of loneliness--no one he started with is still around. After some years, any Crocodile might lose his taste for destroying. The philosophy of dog-eat-dog that served well at the start might be replaced by a depressive phase that requires therapy, in which a review of values becomes a central issue. The excitement for destruction may be refocused into competitive energy, shifting the emphasis from firing people to making dollars.

## Family combats

Those playing the most advanced form of this game usually grew up in families in which there was little or no tender physical contact. The family group was marked by constantly shifting alliances, fights between members, and a pervading combative spirit. Comfort, security, and friendship were secondary to winning family battles.

Typically, a family might have a bitch-mother and a hard-nosed, hard-drinking, macho father. Most of the energy exchanged between the parents is expended in getting back at each other for real and imagined slights. If one is sexually active outside the marriage, the other will repay in kind. Siblings are encouraged to be competitive, one against the other. The parents support their kids in battles with school chums and even teachers. In this household, if a boy comes home after losing a fight to a bigger boy, the father will beat him up and send him back to brain his tormentor.

The combativeness is not confined to family life. During school years, the Crocodile often leads destructive cliques or gangs that prey on other children through physical force and intimidation or swindles. They may also sell drugs of various types.

## The value of predators

Every ecological system requires scavengers to cleanse it of weak animals, carrion, and detritus. Similarly, predators are valuable to keep populations in balance.

For the boss, it's a question of knowing how to manage a Crocodile--how to move him in and out in times of necessity. Learn to keep the Crocodile's predatory activities from decimating the population.

If there's a productive Crocodile who, through tough management supervision, can fit into the company structure, keep him on board. He's a good reserve warrior for a crisis situation.

Remember: You must control him. He can't be allowed to control you.

In a larger corporation, a Crocodile may be kept busy--and also serve management--by being moved from one crisis to another within the organization.

Chapter Three

# MAKING A SCORE

The player is a gambler who loves the long shot, a High Roller who lives for the deal. He goes after a large return from a risky investment even if it means using treachery, artifice, and guile. In business, he is likely to pick the high-risk investment over one with steady, incremental returns. He's a hunch player who isn't exactly sure how he'll get where he wants to go, but lives for the excitement of trying.

## Excitement freak

In fact, the High Roller is so obsessed with excitement as an end in itself that it takes on the power of an addiction; the thrill of the deal is more important than the payoff. The High Roller finds himself needing more and more excitement through risky adventures to satisfy himself. Each new big score is more important and necessary than the last, even if the High

Roller is temporarily successful financially. He will risk all his gains

for each new venture, because, to his venturesome nature, boredom is worse

than insolvency.

Example: The manager of a branch of an antiques store had finally made

his outlet profitable and was about to earn his first year-end bonus. After

months of struggle to bring the branch into the black, the manager had a

bright future with a good salary, bonuses, and an option to buy five percent

of the corporation at a relatively low price. Suddenly, the manager placed

all these gains in hazard. He talked a good customer into bankrolling a new

antiques store that would compete with his present employer, even though

the manager's contract had a specific clause that prohibited him from

opening a rival shop.

He not only gave up his good job, but if his ex-employer enjoined his

business from opening, he risked losing everything. Yet the manager took

the long-odds gamble that the owner wouldn't act against him.

## Going for the long shot

You have two openings in your corporation. One is a steady, permanent

job with a decent salary; the other is a temporary position that has a slim

possibility of becoming an important part of the business. The High Roller

will opt for the long-shot job every time. He prefers the temporary, high-

risk nature of a difficult task over secure employment in a job that is

merely routine.

A High Roller is distinguished from a shrewder entrepreneur by his

self-admitted love of the game. His favorite phrase is, "Hell, it's only

money."

## Brilliant beginnings, but...

Glib and self-confident, the High Roller can talk himself into almost any job situation--and he usually gets off to a flying start. But by checking his references, you'll find that he has a history of successive brilliant beginnings. His strength is the creation of novel enterprises, which he then abandons--often just as they are about to become successful.

Obviously, high risk may also bring outright failure. The work record may also show a history of bankruptcies or other business disasters. The player will use all his verbal skills in explaining these away--they were due to external forces, not his failure of judgment. The truth is, however, that the business troubles were predictable; but the High Roller ignored or overlooked the signs.

## Bragging of beating opponents

A High Roller is easy to diagnose during informal moments. Over a cup of coffee, he will brag of deals pulled off, tricks perpetrated, and how he beat the opposition by shrewd tactics. Always, the emphasis is on the inordinate risks taken: "Boy, that was a close one. I almost got caught, but I managed to pull it off." As he confides this, his glee sparkles in his eyes. He got away with another deal.

A High Roller shows himself in one highly significant way whenever a project of which he is in charge displays signs of becoming successful. He then grows restless and agitated, and starts searching for new ventures that are accompanied by greater risks. Rather than capitalizing and stabilizing his success, he begins to neglect matters for which he is currently responsible.

## The high cost of high rolling

The player's search for excitement carries a price for your company:

* The High Roller initiates extremely risky projects. Even though he is successful in some, the disasters cancel out the gains of the winners.

* Players are volatile, which makes for uncertain relationships with customers. When their deals are threatened in any way, players can stage tantrums--not a way to encourage firm business relationships. By the same token, this instability of temperament means an unsettled relationship between the High Roller and you as boss. The lack of safety and security in his lifestyle spills over into the business.

As he undertakes a new venture, the High Roller sets up an effective network of contacts and customers. His gift of gab and his passion for his project helps him round up interested parties. When it is time for his project to be stabilized and made a part of the institution--the consolidating stages of a sound business--the High Roller pulls out, often disrupting his network of contacts. If he goes into competition with your business, as did the manager of the antiques store, he could carry his best suppliers and customers with him.

## Born wheeler-dealers

In the early phase of a new venture, High Rollers will demonstrate their best efforts, talents, and interests. This talent can be exploited.

Example: A firm has always sold its electronics equipment through middlemen and distributors. Now it wants to experiment with direct marketing. A High Roller is the person to set up the new operation.

High Rollers also make good negotiators if they're backed up by a

tough-minded committee that has final say on contracts. The players are
skilled in negotiations because they're not afraid to try approaches that
wiser heads would reject. And the High Rollers often pull these gambits
off.

Born wheeler-dealers, such players make business deals others can't,
particularly in virgin markets where there are no hard-and-fast guidelines. When new oil money opened up rich markets in the Middle East, the
area was invaded by High Rollers, each with a special scheme. They excel in
jobs that involve trading--coin and stamp sales and collection, antiques,
real estate speculation.

## Turning on with adventure tales

High Rollers are turned on by each other's stories of adventure and
triumph. However, they usually need some hard-working, compliant Mules to
carry their packs and do the routine functions they can't or won't attempt.
These High Roller-Mule relationships have some tension. High Rollers are
soon bored with their Mules and tend to treat them badly after a period of
time.

## A distaste for the ordinary

Players are not good at any job that requires routine, careful record
keeping, or that demand persistent, repetitious effort. Nor do they shine
in positions that are well established and predictable--jobs such as controller, bookkeeper, manager of an already successful outlet, or head of
any division that requires routine, day-to-day overseeing to maintain its
productivity.

High Rollers have problems with excessively cautious bosses. They can produce disasters, however, for those bosses who exercise no control at all.

Example: An aging businessman hired a High Roller to put new spark in his ailing enterprise. The boss gave the player his head and did not watch him. While the boss wasn't looking, the High Roller ran the company into impossible debt with his grand, no-payoff schemes. Each deal sounded great to the High Roller--but none paid back its large investment.

## Good small team players

High Rollers do best with small teams that are highly motivated to conquer new territory. Associates who provide the best support for the player are those who at least echo his enthusiasm for adventure. But they should also be able to do what he can't--keep track of the history of the project so that it's clear what happened, what got spent, and how much the company is likely to realize on its investment.

## Are you a High Roller?

You're an excitement junkie if you're more interested in the thrill of the deal than in making money or being productive. The alternative for you is to become a full-time entrepreneur. This means gambling less and accepting reasonable controls in performance of routine functions. You must learn to stay with a project long enough to exploit it for its full benefit rather than skipping onto the next undertaking. You must also endeavor to settle down and savor the success you've achieved. Don't allow the occasional frustration and boredom of ordinary business life to drive you on

to your next venture before you have had a chance to garner the fruits of
your present labor.

## Two kinds of committed players

There are two types who practice this game in its extreme form:

1. If one of the parents is a High Roller, chances are one of the children will follow suit. In these families, the parents are supportive of the
kid who takes risks.

Example: Dad is a salesman who gambles and indulges in business adventures. He is a great bluffer and in the Friday night card games at home
Dad wins everyone's attention and laughter when he takes the big pot with a
pair of deuces. A child listening would not fail to be impressed.

The child will play cards for money with his friends, trade and hustle
football and baseball cards, and organize games of chance. This is the kid
who takes two newspaper routes, then talks smaller, younger kids into making the rounds while he skims the profits. Later, he might even deal drugs
for the profit involved.

2. The second type of hard-core player comes from a staid, conservative family. Feeling unrewarded or neglected by his parents, a child will
turn to entrepreneurial excitement--the same baseball card hustling and
card games--but in this case as a substitute for the love, care, and affection he's not receiving at home.

As he rejects the starchy, low-energy home folks, the child becomes
an immigrant in the land of adventure. Since this type became a High Roller
without a happy-go-lucky role model, he is more insecure, more compliant
in dealing with authority figures, and more uncertain and aggressive with

peers and competitors than the first type.

## Helping a hard-core player

The problems of the first type are hard to solve because they don't define their behavior as a problem. After all, Dad was a High Roller and so, like as not, was his father before him. The family tree probably has many traders and gamblers on its branches.

No matter how badly these types do, they rarely blame themselves. Occasionally, the brighter ones will become aware that they are more interested in adventure than in accomplishing something lasting. Through self-help books, organizations, or therapy, they may realize the extent of their deep-seated problem. This insight begins the process of learning how to lead a more stable and rewarding life.

Those who become High Rollers in rebellion against staid families may come to psychotherapy for treatment of depression after one of their adventures blows up in their faces. These are more amenable than the happier types to a review and reevaluation of their lives. They often learn how to avoid the cycles of boom or bust both financially and emotionally.

## The need for those who thrive on risks

The High Roller is a crucial part of the free enterprise system. As soon as an opportunity appears, even though unproven and uncertain, the players come crawling out of the woodwork to try it out. Because they are willing to take risks without any guarantees, High Rollers give almost any new idea or process a chance to catch on, and they act as scouts for the entire free enterprise system.

How do they hear of the deals? They invent them, steal them, read about plans for them. They watch for new markets to open. With its oil money, Saudi Arabia built the infrastructure of a modern nation--cities, highways, colleges, desalination plants, water and sewer treatment systems. Most of these enterprises were built by foreigners who were unafraid of risking the clash with local mores and an alien climate to do the job. Some of these High Rollers failed to get started, some went bankrupt, and some made a pile of money.

In the end, High Rollers as speculators provide the liquidity for the stock and commodities markets, and their presence helps make the system work. Often they move in the opposite direction from the general mass of buyers, which provides balance and diversity to investments.

Chapter Four

# TAKING

In contrast to the Crocodile's predatory interest in human flesh and the Paranoid's obsession with getting the SOBs before they get him, the Taker is primarily--though aggressively--self-indulgent. His main concern is having his needs met early and often in matters both large and small.

## A taker's demands

Even before the interview begins, a Taker may manifest himself by requesting or demanding a time that is convenient for him but may be inconvenient for the organization. For example, he might ask for an interview before or after normal business hours so that his current employer won't know that he's job-hunting. Though this is not an unreasonable request, it may be an early warning, especially when weighed with other signs:

• During the interview, the Taker will focus on "What's in it for me?" This interest will extend beyond the normal curiosity of a job applicant. His questions will betray an intense concern with fringe benefits, vacations, chances for advancement, and making sure he receives everything called for by the position.

If the prospective job is difficult, the player will ask about extra compensation, bonuses, obtaining a piece of the company's action. Told the job will require three years before promotion is possible, this applicant might respond, "If I do really well, how can I jump ahead of the others?"

Question him about why he is leaving his current employer at this particular time. You may discover he is abandoning ship at a most inconvenient time--leaving when he's most needed. A Taker will show little concern about such timing. His philosophy is brutally direct: "If you offer me a better deal, I'm yours."

Since he has little concern or empathy for the people he's leaving, chances are he'll ditch your company whenever he gets a better offer--even if that means major inconvenience. Someone who's ambitious but empathetic--and responsible--will arrange his schedule to serve his current employer faithfully, arranging for adequate notice, and working hard right up to the time he departs.

## Looking for preferential treatment

A Taker asks early for special dispensations: "Can I get my first two weeks' pay in advance?" He wants precise answers to his needs--relocation fees paid in advance, any long-term fees or bonuses promised in writing or delivered before they are due. On the other hand, while he demands that his wants be satisfied to the limit, he resists acceptance of any requirement that he inconvenience or even extend himself.

## A claim on prime time

Review vacation schedules in each department. The Takers will have finagled the prime times for themselves. They will also manipulate leave-taking by stringing together vacation and sick-days for extra consecutive time.

Expense accounts also point to Takers: They use the maximum expense allowance, rather than exercising restraint in their outlays of company funds.

If growth brings a stream of new employees into the office, Taker managers will angle for the most skilled and promising workers and the prettiest or handsomest people. This could be true of any alert manager, but while one who is merely ambitious will take into account the feelings of fellow managers, Takers tend to grab anyone or anything they want without considering others.

## Taking means losing money

The selfish behavior of Takers can run up some unnecessary expenses:

• Misallocation of resources can prove costly. A Taker tends to acquire more than his appropriate share of privileges, conveniences, financial and personnel resources.

• The Givers (page 121) in the company are exploited by the Takers, with the accompanying costs of lowered productivity. The Givers become surly and less efficient as the Takers demand more and more without returning payment in kindness or gratitude.

• The Taker's lack of loyalty can hurt the company if he leaves at a time when he is most needed.

• Takers often do no more than the minimum work required; many never live up to their potential.

## Exploiting their exploitive skills

When placed in jobs at the boundaries of the company with the outside world, Takers can turn their exploitive skills to dealing with outsiders rather than fellow employees. They must, however, identify their interests with those of the company. If they do, they make excellent salesmen, recruiters, and negotiators of contracts--positions in which they can spot the weaknesses of others and turn them to the advantage of the company. They are also good at such jobs as that of purchasing agent, where they can talk suppliers down in price. The point is to be certain their natural acquisitiveness works for the organization and is not directed at colleagues.

Takers don't do well in positions demanding extensive dealings with human beings--in personnel, or the direct supervision of line employees. They also fail at delicate negotiations since they tend to be too manipulative and abrupt to stick with long-term, complex dealings.

## Takers and givers

The Takers who make the effort to be agreeable can get along well with Givers who are willing to sacrifice material reward for verbal reinforcement. For example, the Giver will give up his vacation slot to the gracious Taker if he is stroked verbally in return. The Giver then feels he did a good deed, is well loved and cared for, and will be repaid by his fellow worker (the Taker).

## Self-centered aggression

The more ruthless Takers soon exhaust hard-core Givers with their insatiable demands and lack of reciprocity. These Takers also eventually irritate normal, mature people who find their self-centered aggressiveness unpleasant.

## Holding a firm rein

The Taker is such a universal type in business that he appears to fit into many settings where aggressive activity is appropriate--sales, marketing, production--if properly supervised. A prime solution is to hold a firm rein on the Taker so that his drive to grab works to your benefit.

Age works in favor of restraining the Taker. As he accumulates experience, he usually becomes aware that something is wrong; he learns through recurrent negative reactions from people who may have been initially charmed by him. At this stage, the Taker can be amenable to human relations training to increase his awareness and empathy. Through this experience, he may be able to see that less self-centered solutions are more satisfactory from his own point of view than were his more primitive strategies.

## Finding a mentor

Another proven solution for a Taker who has gained some awareness of his problem is a good office relationship with a wiser, more mature person. An ideal combination is an older, chastened Taker who acts as adviser to a younger, less civilized player. When this young Taker runs into problems, the older person serves as role model. As boss, you can match the mentor and a Taker or you can serve as adviser yourself. The idea is to set guidelines for the Taker; and show him when his aggressiveness pays off and when it hurts him--and you--badly.

As in GIVE AWAY, you must make sure that your employees have firm contracts with one another that specify what each person is expected to deliver. Then you should monitor the performance of these contracts to be sure that the Givers aren't exploited and the Takers don't get away with murder.

Remember, milder Takers will back off when confronted with this restrained, businesslike approach.

## The forming of a player

Often the family background of the hard-core player is one of deprivation, with alcoholic parents who can't provide proper food, shelter, and clothing for the kids. Realizing early that he is denied the basics of life by his parents, the player believes that to get what he wants he must take it from someone else.

Some come to this hard-core position from a milder Taker's attitude during periods of business reversal. They are playing an extreme form of the TAKING game called MILK-IT-DRY--the player takes all he can until the goodness he once saw around him has disappeared. Players can fall into MILK-IT-DRY when the company has poor and defeated leadership. If the game is allowed to proceed at the management level, it quickly kills everyone's spirit. The entire business becomes exploitive as it consumes even its own production assets. In this frenzy of grabbing, the motivating conviction is, "If the cats are rats, we might as well all eat cheese."

These extreme players firmly believe that whatever they win, someone else must lose. Thus even the rewards are tainted. But the Milk-It-Drier justifies the grabbing by his conviction that the world is going to the dogs anyway.

## A losing course

Chronic Takers suffer from a serious personality disorder; they should not be hired or, if grave offenders, they should be fired. This is a very depressive game for the hard-core player. Even if the player has the insight to realize that he is on a losing course, he still requires extensive therapy, since the game is rooted in deprivation dating from earliest childhood.

## Civilizing the takers

The aggressive, competitive, self-centered spirit is essential to the entrepreneurial function. The task of management is civilizing the Takers so that they do not consume human resources while being productive.

Chapter Five

# SEXUAL HARASSMENT

Those who play this game turn their power in an organization toward the sexual exploitation of employees. It remains primarily an exercise of male power over female workers, although with more women rising to managerial positions, a few females may also be playing.

Historically, the game has been viewed almost tolerantly. It has been seen as a perquisite of male dominion--the right to harass female workers. The basic assumption is that if the female does not cooperate with the sexual advances of the manager, she can be demoted, passed over for promotions, or even fired.

The game is played at several levels, each of which is sexual in nature. The manager may insist on kissing or fondling the employee in his office. Once this pattern of behavior is established, the game progresses into presexual social interaction. The boss asks the woman for drinks or a meal after work--invitations that are delivered as orders for functions that surpass the normal routine of business activity. Insistence on sexual intercourse and other carnal acts is the next step, often consummated in the office or factory itself. In some businesses, the manager may even order the woman to give her sexual favors to businessmen clients to help the company.

At any stage of the game, the woman is exploited. If she doesn't cooperate, she can lose her job. If she blows the whistle by telling top management, the exploiter will deny it and may try to see to it that she's fired or demoted.

With the growing awareness of the problem faced by women in a business world still dominated by men, females are objecting strenuously to this behavior as a price for employment.

## A leer and a wink

The desire to manipulate power for sexual favors is at least latent in most men. Most successful males learn to control the drive early in their careers, though many still believe that the females at work exist for their benefit. In an interview, they often make that point clear in many subtle-- and not so subtle--ways.

An exploiter will make leering asides about women who are in the room, or about females in general, particularly if he is being interviewed by a man.

Exploiters may be embarrassingly direct. Some will make gratuitous comments about females they have seen while waiting for the interviewer. The boldest might ask a male interviewer point-blank whether he has enjoyed the sexual favors of an attractive woman seated nearby.

When that critical time comes in which the applicant is encouraged to ask questions about the company, the exploiter will inquire about the availability of the women: "Is work all they think about or do they like to have a little fun too?"

## Seeing females as belongings

The player betrays himself by his obsessive talk about physical love. He speaks openly of the women that he has enjoyed and the thrill of the power he feels through this exploitation. He makes it obvious that he regards female employees as chattels.

## Fear, loathing, and a bad example

Few companies can afford a player like this one, who creates such problems as these:

- Fear and poor morale among the women.

- Equally destructive, some women will cater to the player's penchant for sexual conquest and initiate bitter sexual rivalries in the company.

- If the exploiter is allowed to get away with his game, he may be emulated by other managers. This can lead to inadvertent, covert management support for SEXUAL HARASSMENT that can undermine the integrity of the company. Skilled workers of both sexes may resign rather than abide by the unspoken policy.

- The exploiter leaves himself--and the company--open to lawsuits by women who claim to have been harassed.

## Keeping them away from the prey

A known exploiter should never hold any job with unsupervised access to lower-level female employees. This rules out such positions as branch or plant managers in companies such as fast food chains, banks, and light industry that hire many young, inexperienced women. Nor should exploiters be managers of pools of typists, clerks, or secretaries made up primarily of young women.

## Ways to make it stop

The company must unequivocally establish a policy forbidding managers from harassing female workers. This policy must be explicity stated in memos and internal publications; it should also be an unmistakable part of the early training and orientation of new employees. The company must warn any suspected of playing the game that those caught may be fired.

Many companies have created a form of Ombudsman, an officer in the corporation who is specifically assigned to hear grievances about sexual harassment from female workers. Naturally, the Ombudsman's office should be a safe haven where employees can talk about their difficulties, and where they know that what they say will be held in the strictest confidence. This procedure is being tested by the federal government for its women employees. Like any organization, the feds have male exploiters and the Ombudsman's office is a place where women can register their complaints and expect a fair hearing. The purpose of this Ombudsman's office is twofold:

1. It is an authorized place to file charges against an exploiter. Repeated or continued allegations and proven acts could lead to his dismissal.

2. It protects the women from the consequences of having refused the advances of the exploiter--and of reporting him to his superiors.

## A severe shortage of self-esteem

The extreme forms of the game are based on male inadequacy, a belief by the player that he's only safe when he has complete power over women. He dreads the risk of approaching a woman of equal power who could rebuff him. He must, therefore, lord it over the women under his command.

As he grows older, the player may encounter a variety of sexual problems based on his underlying doubts about his adequacy. Primary among these is impotence, which, in this form, can generally be helped only through extensive psychotherapy.

The company's stance toward the hard-core player must be unyielding. The worst offenders must be told to seek professional help. Those who refuse are to be segregated from the civilized society of the business community.

## The distinction between harassment and flirting

Innocent sexual play, such as flirting and "kidding around" between males and females, is one of the pleasures of working. It can be a delightful social lubricant if kept to a first-degree level by a carefully formulated company policy rooted in orientation, training, and supervision. The game is only fun, however, as long as the lower-level female employees are secure in the knowledge that the "playing around" will not devolve into exploitation.

Chapter Six

# COWBOY

He--and often she--rides into your business acting as if just off the open range--solitary, independent, strong-willed. If he sees a challenge that appeals to him, he'll settle down for a while and work hard and well. He stays until he grows restless--usually long enough to earn some money and keep his career moving. But the wanderlust proves irresistible and soon he travels on.

He's not a real screen Cowboy; he only acts like one. To him, a job in a company is like a puncher's trip into town to earn a grubstake, fix his saddle, buy a new blanket, and have a few drinks. Almost every business has examples of such people, particularly among its younger employees. In fact, at least in spirit, most boys want to grow up to be a Cowboy. He is the American folk hero and his attitudes are by no means restricted to the Wild West.

## A rough-and-ready approach

He dresses to suit himself. Unlike other job candidates, he won't wear a standard three-piece interview uniform.

He tends to have rough-and-ready habits. Often he is bluff, hardy, and laconic. His approach is, "You tell me what you want me to do and I'll listen. If it's something I'm willing to try, I'll do it. If not, I won't."

He is relatively uncompromising during the interview. He reminds you constantly of his independence and his unquestioned ability to make it on his own. If hired, he'll say when he's ready to come on board. If that doesn't suit you--well, he didn't need the job that badly anyway.

The Cowboy's job history is a giveaway of his game. While it shows one exciting assignment after another, there is little continuity. Even if he worked productively for the same person for ten years, it was probably in bursts of six months at a time.

## A stance apart from the group

A Cowboy talks, dresses, and acts independently. He sets himself apart from the crowd through his personal stances and inability to run with the herd. He does not get stampeded into the latest fads and causes, nor is he particularly active in office politics. He goes his own way.

Self-assured and proud, he reacts negatively to criticism, constraint, and control.

The Cowboy generally has no interest in promotion or advancement. To him, the most alluring assignments are high-paying, with solitary duties or functions. He will often only work on a team made up of other Cowboys who are attempting a difficult or challenging task--prospecting or drilling for oil, for example.

## Paying the player's price

A Cowboy is expensive to corral--you must lure him with dollars and freedom. Thus, not only is his salary costly, but the independence you grant him also encourages other employees to seek his privileges.

If the Cowboy does a good job, the company will suffer a difficult withdrawal period when he decides to leave. He may have been expensive, but he is hard to replace. Also there are the psychological costs of losing a skilled worker and the feelings of longing his departure brings to the former (or would-be) Cowboys who remain behind.

When the Cowboy's wandering instincts are thwarted, he can grow abrasive. He may inspire mutiny among his fellow employees if the company is experiencing difficult times. The costs of this rebellion can range from decreased productiviity and morale to outright work stoppages. Leading office revolutions is the main interest of Cowboys; however, this cost is rare and usually not severe.

Any pursuits that are routine, static, and control-oriented, such as the jobs of bookkeeper or filing clerk, are anathema to a Cowboy. Occasionally, his lack of conventional job skills may force him to take jobs that demand predictable behavior--for example, waiter or assistant manager in a fast food outlet. But these positions seldom work out for the Cowboy or his boss.

A Cowboy can have trouble finding his exact niche. He is often over-qualified and not amenable to the precise schedules of most jobs.

A Cowboy can't abide pomposity or posturing, or anyone that is straitlaced, compulsive, or detail-oriented. Unfortunately, this list of attributes describes many members in good standing of civilized society.

## A loner's interest

A player gets along best with other Cowboys--they know how to leave him alone. He can deal with a tough-minded range-boss who can direct and drive a Cowboy on the job yet still allow him free rein. The Cowboy will respect anyone who trusts him enough to give him an assignment, then turns him loose without too much checking, pestering, or supervision.

## Skilled itinerant workmen

Cowboys with the best work records are in professions that tolerate periodic job changes--sales, advertising, journalism, troubleshooting. In short, they take well to any job in which a tendency to wanderlust is covered by the nature of the business.

Don't fight his wanderlust. The first signs are his shift from an involved, dedicated worker to one who suddenly fails to show up. He becomes increasingly restive and irritable as he undergoes the transformation from Town Cowboy to Train Cowboy. When this happens, encourage him to move on, but make it clear he will be welcome back the next time he wants work.

## No role modeling

Encourage your employees to accept the Cowboy as an exception in the business world. Try not to let the rest of the office think of the Cowboy as a model, especially in his independent way of approaching his task. Most of the work done in a company demands close teamwork. If everyone were Cowboys, few business functions could be accomplished.

## The Cowboy in the boss

Cowboys don't run organizations. But many bosses have some Cowboy in them, or they may have been players when younger. If so, their problem can lie in dealing with occasional bouts of wanderlust that can make the reformed Cowboy want to dump all the things he works for and ride off into the sunset. If you are afflicted, one way to improve matters is to give in (a little) and guarantee yourself periodic vacations. You can also diversify your life by having several different projects going on at once so that the routine doesn't become stifling. Don't allow the life of your successful organization to impose a stultifying regime on your life; this can push you into the wanderlust phase of the Cowboy game.

## As kids, adventuresome brats

Players of the game in its third-degree form grew up as aggressive, adventurous brats. Usually the fathers were also Cowboys; female Cowboys were tomboys who were encouraged by their parents to be venturesome and independent while avoiding passive, feminine roles. Both male and female players took pride in the game and were backed with parental support.

## Working with hard-core players

• Being a Cowboy is a lifelong affliction for extreme practitioners. Very few therapists are fast or tough enough to lasso a Cowboy in order to help him solve his problem--unwillingness to stay put.

• The only time a Cowboy will discuss solutions is when he wants to marry, or when a return of the wanderlust threatens to break up a settled existence.

During these times a therapist-consultant can talk with a Cowboy about his priorities. He must find a balance between adventure, wanderlust, and excitement on the one hand, and a desire for a family with the roots of a settled life on the other. Since the two lifestyles are essentially opposed, the balance is often tough to strike. Most successfully settled Cowboys have taken ingredients from both lives--enough wandering and adventure to satisfy the Cowboy side and a rooted life with a loving family to take care of his need for stability.

## Virtues of the Cowboy code

Cowboys are needed in business to take on the difficult tasks that most other people don't have the gumption to do.

The settled-down Cowboy is one of America's ideal types--our heroes are modeled after him. He's a standup guy who takes no guff from anybody. He goes to work and does his job without complaining. He doesn't let competitors push him around, yet he is honorable. He's direct, a man of his word who never lies and does what he says. He is unafraid to confront the boss when he stands in opposition to a policy, yet can also admit it when he has made a mistake. He treats others fairly and never willfully hurts anyone, except sometimes in retaliation when he is hurt himself. He stays out of your business but will help out gladly when asked.

What's wrong with a Cowboy? Not much--as long as you know how to persuade him to serve your company with all his positive attributes.

Chapter Seven

# HAVE I GOT A DEAL FOR YOU

Some people always have a bargain they want to share with you. Unsolicited, they will approach you with an offer that supposedly will save you big money. The player's opening words are something like, "Have I got a deal for you!"

Trouble is, the deal seldom materializes in the proposed form. Either crucial terms have been omitted from the initial discussions or the costs have been misrepresented. Some flaw usually renders the deal unfeasible-- no matter how tempting it sounds.

Example: The boss of a small plastics corporation wants to build a light manufacturing plant in a convenient suburb. His assistant, who is conducting the site search, meets Bill, a fellow member of the Lions Club, who claims to have the perfect site. The land is readily attainable, according to Bill, with just a slight zoning variance.

After visiting the site, the boss and his assistant realize its potential: the land meets all their requirements--railroad frontage, good drainage, accessibility. Not only that, Bill claims the land can be had for a song. It's owned by a widow who wants to sell it off and retire. And, Bill himself is executor of the estate controlling the land. Bill crows, in effect, "Have I got a deal for you!"

## The hassle surfaces

One small hitch--that zoning variance. The boss believed Bill when he said it was a mere formality; he plunked down a chunk of money as a binder on the land. But when the boss and assistant appear before the zoning board to request the variance, the very mention of the site stirs angry mutterings. Arguments over the zoning classification have raged for years. The issue divides the townspeople and board into warring factions, both of which have disavowed compromise.

So begins what could be years of hearings, meetings, and court fights. The plastics company expends thousands of dollars and wastes hundreds of fruitless hours. The lawyers' fees alone add up to a small fortune. All the while, Bill stands by watching the company fight his zoning battle with its money. When and if the property is ever cleared he'll sell it off and take the profit. But for the boss, the dream deal looms as a nightmare.

## Basic foulups

To be gulled into playing HAVE I GOT A DEAL FOR YOU, the gullible boss must make two mistakes in judgment:

1.  He must believe that the player, Bill in our story, is really Santa

Claus who wants only to give a present. This game only works when the boss is convinced that a stranger will enter his life bearing a gift.

2. The boss must neglect to check the facts as espoused by the player. Invariably, the most routine checking reveals that the game is in progress --the flaws are all there to be seen if only the boss or his staff takes the time to investigate.

In this story, a simple reading of past zoning board records and minutes of their meetings would have bared the controversy surrounding the site. Bill's assurances of an easy zoning variance would have been exposed as the statements of convenience uttered by a dedicated player.

## A seductive manner

Don't be seduced by the Dealmaker's pleasant manner; he is by nature affable, enthusiastic, and optimistic. He greets you like a long-lost friend, even if you've never met before.

Never forget that the deal is being presented in glowing terms with every possible defect going unmentioned. Those problems that do surface are spoken of offhandedly and then discounted quickly as being only minor irritations.

Don't fall for this line; question the Dealmaker assiduously about all the negative factors. If you persist in pinning him down, he may become vague or try to change the subject. This is a sure sign that he is glorifying the deal.

He signals another warning to you when he stiff-arms any verification of his facts. "Your people will be misled by what they hear," he'll say. "I know all you need to know on this deal. Trust me." Whenever a Dealmaker tells you not to double-check his facts, show him the door.

## A cozy venality

Find out what's in it for him. Most Dealmakers minimize their personal profit and act as though they want the deal out of altruism. Bill supposedly wanted to help the widow, since he was executor of her husband's estate--and he wanted to help his fellow Lions Club member find the perfect site. The fact that Bill would have a zoning problem solved by an outside party and make a profit in the bargain was never mentioned.

Dealmakers also try to make themselves cozy with you by admitting their venality. "I'll make a killing on this deal," one might say. "But so will you." This form of negative ingratiation often reassures the boss that as long as profits are made, the deal must be sound. Be leery of this tactic--if anyone makes a killing, it's usually only the Dealmaker.

But why go through all this with a person you don't basically trust? Why not just throw him out the door before he begins his pitch? The answer is deceptively simple: He may actually have a deal for you. Not all Dealmakers lie all the time; occasionally one may get lucky and have something that's to your advantage.

Similarly, though the deal may not be as attractive as advertised, with careful investigation it might be remolded to suit your needs. Any Dealmaker deserves a respectful--and skeptical--hearing. You never know how his ideas might be useful to your business.

Occasionally, a Dealmaker will be one of your managers or employees who brings in a proposition from an outside source. This in-house Dealmaker should not be exempted from the same scrutiny given the outsider.

Even a respected employee can't be trusted implicitly. He may be blind to the negative features of the deal because he wants to curry favor or make a name by doing something good for the company.

Warning: If the Dealmaker is a friend or trusted associate, this game is a guaranteed relationship-breaker. For that reason alone, all deals offered by those people important to you--friends, relatives, close business colleagues--must be carefully considered. A sour deal may cost you more than money.

## Sellers with a mission

Working directly for you, Dealmakers have their uses. They are good idea men, even though only one in ten of their schemes is valid. They are so enthusiastic and optimistic, and they search so hard for the special possibility that can be transformed into a profitable enterprise, that they are often worth having around. They are born salesmen who are particularly skilled at cold-canvass--people who work from door-to-door or on the phone selling products to strangers who have no initial interest.

When you are trying to move goods that have suffered from strong buyer resistance, the player of this game is your man. A player may also be gifted at selling off used equipment of little current value.

Conversely, players are excellent scavengers when you need usable secondhand plant equipment or office furniture. They can scrounge up whatever is needed at a low price or through elaborate bartering.

## Undependable managers

Dealmakers should never be left to their own devices. They serve the company best on a team where someone more stable and cautious reviews the details after the player has blazed the trail by putting together a deal.

Thus, they are not reliable as foremen or creative group heads. Nor should they be placed in charge of isolated branches or district offices. They're not dependable plant or store managers because they'll spend more time making deals than they will on any other company business.

## Supervision is the key

Place the player under the management of a practical, scrupulous supervisor who can properly investigate the deals as they are proposed and segregate the feasible from the impossible.

## The origins of the urge

Players tend to grow up in families where beating the system is admired. As children the players believe that they'll discover the way to make it all work for them--even though their parents tried and failed. If Daddy was an alcoholic, or any other type who can't make a deal with life, the player sets out to prove that he can do better. Unfortunately, he discovers as Daddy did that you can't beat life--you learn to live with it. But because making deals is so much a part of our culture, the player seems to be displaying normal behavior--it's unusual that he'll seek aid for his problem because he doesn't know he has one. Even when a third-degree player suffers a long string of bad deals, his behavior is not always viewed as pathological in a business environment. Often, the failures are attributed to a lack of luck or external circumstances, such as a recession.

Dealmakers occasionally have their world collapse around them, how-

ever, and the resulting shock plunges them into depression. At these vulnerable times they may seek counseling--or will be receptive to suggestions for professional aid.

Often aging is the best cure. As some players grow older they find that
the drive to beat the system diminishes. They lose their extravagant
outlook and tone down their behavior.

Many a Dealmaker can be brought around by a strong entrepreneur who
can reshape the player through example and direction. This mentor can keep
the player within the limits of common sense as he channels his enthusiasm,
vision, and thirst for deals toward those that have the highest chance of
success. Under this guidance, a higher percentage of the deals will be
brought to fruition and the player will shift from addicted Dealmaker to
respected entrepreneur.

## Sometimes it's a stage

Dealmaking is often the first step on the way toward becoming a sharp
entrepreneur. A person who's a Dealmaker in his 20's might well become a
prosperous businessman in his 30's and 40's. The point is to avoid the fool-
hardy, no-chance deals while maintaining the excitement of the chase.

The wonderful part about the Dealmaker is that he will sometimes un-
cover a possibility that others weren't sharp enough to see. He is out there
in the marketplace turning over every rock in his search for the golden
worm. Since there is a golden worm under every hundred-thousandth rock,
sooner or later the Dealmaker will find it.

Chapter Eight

# SWEATHOG

Competent, often extremely able, a Sweathog* is proud of his failings. He revels in his negative attributes--an impoverished background, ignorance, lack of social graces or manners. Instead of trying to play down his disadvantages, he proclaims them loudly as announcements of his triumph. He can be a severe trial. Among the varieties of Sweathog are:

• The roughneck oil millionaire who strides the plush corridors of his company's skyscraper headquarters attired on old work clothes, beat-up field boots, and sun-bleached 10-gallon hat. He swaggers about his achievements while deliberately using the untutored accent and blunt, limited vocabulary of a person who never went beyond grammar school.

• The ex-convict who rose above his adversity to attain a respected

*The word "Sweathog" comes from the popular TV situation comedy, Welcome Back, Kotter. In the show, the Sweathog is portrayed as a loud but endearing person who is flawed but has a lot of rough virtue.

position in a growing corporation. Dressed in a $400 suit at a high-level policy meeting, he always has a tale or two to tell about his days in prison.

• The cool veteran of a childhood in the inner city, who through grit and drive rises to the boardroom of a wealthy company. The Sweathog delights in slipping into the street vernacular of his youth--to the embarrassment of other board members, who may feel put down and put off.

Sweathogs feel that by leading with their weaknesses--coarse language, off-beat behavior--they are saying, "This is the way I am, take it or leave it." Many players also make light of their failings so that others will be able to laugh them off.

While justifiably proud of his achievements, the Sweathog genuinely feels inferior to those from more affluent backgrounds. He flaunts his deficiencies in behavior that is a form of overcompensation for his sense of inadequacy and his fear of rejection. His talk and behavior can make business relations strained, especially as the player frequently rises to the levels of management where executives prefer to keep their minds on business, not games.

While the game can be crippling, it does have its rewards. Keeping company among his betters enables the player to boast, "I'm just a Sweathog, but look how high I've risen. I may not be smooth, but, by God, I've made something of my life." Such feelings of well-being temporarily override the basic moods of inadequacy persistently experienced by the player.

## Check out the whole background

When approaching a company for a job, a Sweathog is usually obvious--he's gross.

A Sweathog may arrive with a rave recommendation from a friend or business acquaintance. But there will often be a reservation that goes something like this: "He's a great guy and good worker, just don't be put off by his...." The rest of the sentence will warn of his "frank language," or penchant for talking about his shady past.

The smarter heads can disguise their Sweathog orientation during an interview. The background can often only be uncovered through a careful check of job references: look for blanks in the resume that could mean years spent out of work while serving time in prison; make sure the education record is not pure fabrication; be alert for any comments by former employers or colleagues about lack of social graces or difficulties in handling personal relationships. You should know the complete background of a suspected Sweathog, however, so that he can never surprise you with his history at a time when you don't want to hear about it, as in the midst of an important company meeting or party.

## The best uses of a basically good employee

Players take hold of any task that benefits from their determination and shrewdness, including such basic areas of business as sales, production, marketing. They can make good entrepreneurs, particularly in fields such as heavy construction, refuse collection, sand and gravel pit operation.

To enable associates to adjust to the Sweathog, allow him to play his game while assuring his colleagues that he is competent. Remind associates that you are paying him for his capacity to produce and not his manners. Ask only that they share your tolerance of his rough edges.

## Polishing the rough diamond

In the musical <u>My Fair Lady</u>, the aristocratic language professor, Henry Higgins, transformed Liza Doolittle from a street flower-girl into a lady who was accepted as a person of breeding and social refinement. You, as boss and adviser, can change a Sweathog from a social deadbeat to a winner. Your hardest job, however, will be to convince the player that he should change. He'll fight it--because as he sees it, he has succeeded by bucking the current. But once the Sweathog accepts the principle, he'll be a fast learner. The specific steps for leading a player into polite society can be summarized. Persuade him to:

• Enroll in college courses--write some papers, speak up in classes, have the experiences in higher classroom education that he may have missed along the way.

• Undertake a reading program that can be either self-directed or guided by someone he knows and trusts. Reading can be anything above his current level--including some classics.

• Seek the aid of a personal consultant who works with him directly rather than through the company. The consultant must be someone, probably a psychotherapist, who can help him face the issues of his fears and feelings of inadequacy. This consultant may also supply directions for reading and learning programs.

## One cure: flight

The Sweathog game is full of ironies, however. For example, if you succeed in transforming your Sweathog into a social human being, you run the risk of driving him from the company.

Remember: The original issue is the Sweathog's lack of self-esteem. In order to overcome this game, he must bare his soul by admitting his background and the ways he has adopted to mask his sense of inadequacy. The agony of self-examination may force him to flee. Once reformed, he may feel that work in a place where he is unknown as a former Sweathog is his only viable solution.

Thus a full-scale change may lose you a good employee. The gain for the Sweathog, however, is solid: his game won't recur. Once purged, he's forever free. If he does stay on, he can advance in your company through his genuine dedication to work--much happier in the knowledge that his game is over.

## A question for the boss

If you're a top manager and feel you're a Sweathog, you are free to continue the game--you're in charge. But the nagging question remains: Have you been paying an unnecessarily high price for carrying on as you do?

If the answer is yes, then you should consider applying--for yourself--the reeducation techniques discussed above.

Chapter Nine

# EMPEROR

Charismatic and strong-willed, the leader of an organization, often its founder, constructs his domain through sheer force of will, supported by acuteness of business judgment. His personality is so strong and his grasp of the business so sound that he takes on the aura of an Emperor, especially among his most loyal employees.

In time, however, the Emperor becomes infatuated with being worshipped, and his effectiveness diminishes. He is so wrapped up in his role that he begins to devour the resources he created. Business gains are sacrificed if they impair his Emperor's image, and ill-considered projects are undertaken if they hold promise of adding to his grandeur. Eventually, this once-dynamic, innovative leader wears out his organization's resources; the company is ravaged by the depredations of a tyrant's megalomania.

The game of EMPEROR is an occupational hazard of any energetic, effective top executive. Although in its later stages the game manifests itself through the regal strutting of the player, its beginnings are subtle. A player seldom realizes when he starts to play. Managers slipping into the game ignore friendly warnings, convinced that they alone know what's best for the company and its workers.

When the Emperor can no longer be confronted, the game is in full control of the player. Now the Emperor is deaf to words of advice and warning offered by managers and employees. Trapped in a sense of his own infallibility, the Emperor is consumed by his vision of an empire in which he will reign as a benevolent despot over forever grateful subjects. In this state, the Emperor has turned a principal asset of his company--his strong character and executive ability--into a stark liability.

## The embryo emperor

An Emperor-to-be usually starts off working for someone. In fact, his first empire may be your business--after he assumes control. So watch for these signs that warn of an incipient player:

• A future Emperor comes on as the perfect employee for an entrepreneurial organization. He is intelligent, aggressive, results-oriented, and often has a history of having overcome a difficult childhood in order to be successful.

• His work history usually reveals a string of dazzling successes, some against overwhelming odds. He's one of those businessmen with the skills and instincts to change a losing situation into a winning one. Fellow workers might say of him, "He can fall into a cesspool and come up with a rose between his teeth."

He is a born entrepreneur, but the telltale signs of the EMPEROR game include an excessive interest in control, a thirst for independence, and a dislike of teamwork. A would-be player demands minimum supervision and rejects any interference once his plan of action has been approved. He might say to a boss, "You leave me alone on the job, and I'll show you some results."

## Angling for the big one

Even in the early phases of his game, the future Emperor always opts for the grandiose plan. He insists on managing the big job, the difficult assignment that other managers shy away from. To prove himself supremely capable, he willfully crosses that fine line between high ambition and overweening drive. He will not be denied.

Example: A business problem has frustrated a company's managers and division heads for months. While ideas have been plentiful at brainstorming sessions, the answer remains elusive. Finally, a consensus emerges that the problems are, indeed, unsolvable. But the future Emperor rejects such conclusions. He spends nights and weekends in seclusion, perhaps even takes some vacation days to free his thoughts. At last, he appears in your office with a gleam of triumph in his eye and a workable plan that solves the problem.

## Against all odds

Thus, while the future Emperor gives much to the company, he does incur some real risks, particularly in the role of leader:

• His penchant for grand projects can be expensive. In his later stages he delights in enterprises in areas where the company has no expertise or previous experience. He may take a manufacturing company into land speculation, for example. Or he may transform a supply company into a manufacturing outlet that sells its own product through direct marketing. The odds against the success of such endeavors is staggering; some take the marketplace by storm, but the great majority are--or can be--abysmal failures.

• While an ordinary entrepreneur will weigh the pros and cons of a business venture, the Emperor will often simply plunge ahead. His supreme self-confidence makes him view the risks as a challenge. Not only can his schemes cost the company money, but they may frighten away would-be partners or investors and give the firm an unwanted reputation as reckless and unreliable.

If the leader's ambition is viewed as irrational, many of the best most sensible employees will leave the company. When the Emperor becomes nonconfrontable, the only employees who remain will be the scared and sycophantic--workers whose competence is less important to the company than their loyalty.

• As terminal grandiosities deplete and exhaust the resources of the company, the game can lead to bankruptcy, takeover, or, in the case of nonprofit organizations, dissolution. (This cost is akin to the devastating price paid by France for Napoleon's disastrous invasion of Russia.)

• The saddest cost to the Emperor and the company is that his hypercompetent, ambitious entrepreneur has lost the opportunity to realize his plans and leave a legitimate mark on the business world.

## Able, imaginative power wielders

Future Emperors are so accomplished they can perform well at almost any task. They tend, however, to gravitate toward jobs in which they can wield power while exercising creativity and initiative. As extremely able administrators when the game is in its formative stages, they are skilled at operating branches, franchises, and divisions. In any military-style operation, they are the stuff of which generals are made.

Imperial operators may turn mutinous if subjected to routine jobs performed under excessive supervision. They will also rebel against jobs in which opportunities are restricted. To take some suitable examples, Emperors aren't the ones to manage dry-cleaning establishments, laundries, or the local supermarket.

## Persuasive manipulators

With their magnetic personalities, these players are unsurpassed at manipulating interpersonal relationships. Not only can they get along with almost anyone, they can induce rational people to follow them enthusiastically into harebrained schemes. Emperors have often led their own and others' businesses down the road to ruin while raising toasts to their projected success.

## Keeping the game under control

In business, Emperors can only assume complete control over wobbly structures. They have little luck in taking over smoothly functioning companies--or governments. The best hedge against an Emperor's takeover, therefore, is to keep your business structurally sound. If conditions do slip temporarily, beware of the dynamic, aggressive manager who assures you he can solve all your problems. At the first sign of hesitancy, this incipient Emperor will seize his opportunity--and try to grab your company.

Under solid management, future Emperors can be deflected from their game through a process of civilization. This means that you must exert all your efforts toward teaching the player to concentrate his prodigious energies on feasible plans. Strong mentorship by you, or an established leader in your company, can guide the player away from the pitfalls of the game. If you feel you need help, consultations between the player and an outside professional therapist may be in order. With the proper direction, the incipient Emperor can develop into a candidate for top manager. Just be sure he isn't seduced by his own unrealistic schemes.

## Standing up to the Emperor

One of the strengths of an Emperor is that he is almost always right-- at least about business. (Only in his later, irrational stages does he undertake the grand plans that are so fraught with danger and potential failure.) It's sometimes hard, therefore, to encourage his associates to stand up to him. On top of this, the dazzling persuasiveness of his personality reinforces his capable arguments.

Though fellow executives may lack his vision, they must be backed up when they register their reservations. Often, these checks on the Emperor are the only influences that keep his game within bounds.

Remember: The Emperor enters into the final, catastrophic phases of his game when he is no longer confrontable. Just as colleagues must never stop confronting an Emperor, he should never be allowed to shut down two-way communication. They must speak up and he must be receptive.

## The best for the boss

Since many gifted founders and entrepreneurs fall prey to this game, you could be a player--or a future player--without realizing it. Customarily, the Emperor doesn't seek aid until he is in the terminal stages. Even then, he has a tendency to blame his troubles on external forces or a lack of zeal on the part of members of his coterie.

When he is in the terminal stages and unapproachable by his own employees, any consultant hired is led on by the Emperor. Then he is chewed up by the Emperor's manipulations and spat out. For some consultants, the high fee charged may make it worthwhile to be masticated. But for the Emperor, little relief from his game comes from this behavior.

In this late phase, the only solution for the Emperor--assuming that he has the objectivity to seek help of any kind--is to hire a therapist who can outfox, outmaneuver, and out-think the player. This type of practitioner is rare, because he is the very best.

Many children believe that if they could create a world they controlled, all their dreams could come true and they'd be content. Someone who plays the EMPEROR game in the third degree is a child to attempts to mold such a world. He believes that by forming this ideal realm, he'll be forever served by loyal and grateful retainers (his employees).

To create this ideal, the Emperor trades on his talents and aggressions and the willingness of some employees to engage in TRUE BELIEVER (see page 130). At first, the organization is a winning entrepreneurial venture. Then, after many successes, the rot creeps in as the leader takes on

70

the attitudes and trappings of Emperor.

Since the empire is the product of the Emperor's mind, employees have difficulty initiating the confrontations that hold the player under control. Unchecked, the Emperor becomes a tyrant who destroys his own creation with his glorious--but ruinous--plans.

# Chapter Ten

# TERRITORY

Most of the other games in this book are played by a single disturbed worker. This one falls into a special category, however, since we all carry the seeds of territoriality in our genes. It is a game--another name for it is war--that each of us plays at one time or another; but in this case we will discuss what happens when it occurs in a business setting.

Factories and offices are commonly organized in divisions that handle separate functions of the business--e.g., production, shipping, mail, sales, and so on. To be truly efficient, a business is absolutely dependent on harmonious relationships between these various sections.

## A state of hostilities

Frequently, however, feuds erupt between divisions--squabbles based on territorial dynamics. When each section starts defending its territory against the others, the business is in a state of conflict that can lead to its destruction.

In TERRITORY, each division blocks and delays transactions and treats "outsiders" from other divisions as enemies. The divisions even refuse to learn one another's language; they will not make the effort to understand what the "enemy" is trying to communicate. New terms or concepts introduced by another group are rebuffed as intrusions.

Even though the divisions are in the same company, supposedly dedicated toward the same profit goals, each derives actual joy from the embarrassments and difficulties of the others. Requests for assistance and cooperation are scorned as each camp holds the others in the contemptuous regard reserved for bitter foes.

To grasp the concepts of TERRITORY, we must realize that humans have two ways of relating to territory--as held in common or as privately owned.

1. Held in common. Territory can be owned jointly by the people using it. In a well-organized business, each section is occupied and utilized by different workers, who claim their divisions as their territories. Yet they recognize that in case of conflict, their claims are superseded by the demands of the company; the territories are held in common for the benefit of the corporation.

2. Privately owned. Territory is often claimed by those who mark it as their private domain and then are willing to defend it against intruders. This private concept of territory inspires some of the deepest passions in the natural world. Certain mammals, such as the wolf, delineate their areas by urinating or leaving glandular secretions, the scents from which warn rivals that the land is claimed. Through these intimate ac-

tions, they announce to the world that this given patch of territory is theirs. Many animals, including man, will stake out their personal realms and then risk life and limb in their defense.

## Friendly rivalry: A benefit

Every boss encourages competition between divisions--it can push each to greater heights. This rivalry, however, should not extend past the amiable bantering level of a softball game.

The best way to pick up signs that real territorial feuds are developing between divisions is to chat with managers and employees during their relaxed times such as lunch or coffee breaks. Be alert for rabid outbursts: "Those SOB's in sales aren't holding up their end. We're making a great product, but we don't have half the sales figures we should have. If they don't start selling more, they should be fired."

## Dispersion can be a factor

Territoriality often flourishes in a corporation that has a central office with outlying divisions. Everything that goes wrong in the divisions is blamed on the central office. The outposts complain that the central headquarters understands nothing about local conditions and that the board of directors is too removed from their daily operations. It takes little for branch offices to declare war against their own headquarters in the same way that provinces will turn against those in authority in the capital of their mother country. Similarly, insensitive headquarters will fight back in kind. They will brand the branches provincial, staffed with hicks who don't understand modern business procedures. If headquarters sent saboteurs to damage the machinery in its own divisions it couldn't do more harm to the corporation.

## The game out of control

Once TERRITORY is rampant in a company, it is almost impossible to stamp out. Even if the managers and crews who started it are all replaced, the game continues to rule. It becomes part of the "culture" of each division; branch offices can't stand headquarters, for example; sales loathes production and vice versa. And the employees go along because their need for private territory promotes a loyalty to their immediate group that overrides any sense of commonality as an employee of the company.

One obvious price you can pay for allowing this game to take hold and flourish is the destruction of your company. Short of that, however, there are other wastages:

- The crushing costs of a civil war--including lasting bitterness.
- The undermining, over the long term, of projects dependent on cooperation.

Example: Because sales and production are feuding and will not coordinate with each other, a company can't satisfy its current customers by delivering goods that have been ordered. This means that the salesmen can't expand into new territories--they haven't even been able to supply those customers who are already signed on. Conversely, production may feel it is exacting revenge on the sales division by not supplying them with goods to sell. In the same way, a company with a strong production team can manufacture more goods than are being sold. The sales force could be slowing down just to watch the gang in production stew in their own juices.

• A diversity of divisional languages and "cultures" means that executives promoted to the corporate management level from one section will make unnecessary mistakes concerning the others--all because they lack basic information and understanding.

## Prevention is the cure

If ever a game could be stopped before it starts, it is this one. To keep your company from breaking up into warring territories, follow these steps:

• Maintain open lines of communication between divisions.

• Any conflicts between managers or members of their group must be resolved quickly through negotiations. Don't allow resentments to simmer.

• Cross-train managers so that the group heads understand the relationship of each division to the company as a whole.

• Hold regular meetings of division managers in which joint decisions are made and enforced. These meetings must persistently stress the concept of cooperation and coordination between each group.

• Make it clear that your company does not encourage the playing of TERRITORY. State this position publicly and frequently.

## Police action

In spite of all efforts, the game may still break out--at any time. If so, the fastest universal solution is to do as the European kings did in ending the feudal rule of their nobles--collect all the power from the division managers. You may need the help of an outside consultant, but here's what you can do on your own:

• Take hold. No division must be allowed to operate autonomously. Each must be under your control, no matter how specialized its job happens to be.

• Be sure division managers see each other as human beings who are members of the same company, not hostile leaders of rival tribes.

• Hold regular, interdivisional meetings to indoctrinate the managers in the basic concepts of commonality. Attendance must be mandatory. Do not let any manager believe that the rules don't apply to him. Stick to these meetings religiously--it is not time wasted.

Once your top managers have been persuaded of the notion that they are cooperating for the general good, institute a plan with each that passes along these lessons to their workers. Here's a sample plan:

• Hold discussion groups among workers to accomplish what similar talks did with the managers. Remind the workers that their future lies with the company, not in loyalty to a division or its leader.

• Cross-train by transferring workers between divisions.

• Sponsor social events that involve members of two or more divisions.

• Have your division heads include workers in the decision-making process to promote harmony between divisions. Do this by having managers consult strong members from the work force to try and reach a consensus for each interdivisional decision.

This program will take time--perhaps a year or more until the hostilities are finally eliminated between divisions. While most employees will be retrainable, some may have to be let go if the game is so ingrained that they can't abandon it.

Warning: Some bosses are blind to the line between friendly competition and TERRITORY. It's all right to encourage sales and production to outdo one another for the greater good of the company. But if the boss starts playing one division off against the other in a territorial conflict, then he has a problem. A boss who has to divide to conquer obviously feels inadequate about his ability to manage. He needs the professional help of a therapist.

## Wolves and sheep

Humans can be either herd animals or carnivores hunting in small packs--sheep and wolves. Sheep aren't territorial, but survive on herd instincts; wolves are highly territorial, with strict ways of maintaining the life of the pack.

The problem in business is that the most aggressive, ambitious entrepreneurs are wolves. They are uncomfortable being sheep and existing in herd-communal situations. They have an enormous personal inborn drive to have their own ingroup, their clique, their pack, and then to mark off the territory in which each functions best. They'll even go to war to create or maintain territory.

Since some of the most accomplished businessmen are wolves, they will naturally fall into territoriality even if it's not in the best interests of the organization. The successful manager, then, must know when to be a sheep and when to be a wolf; he must know when to share territory for the sake of cooperation and when to protect it in the face of a  legitimate threat.

The essence of the free enterprise capitalistic system is the competitive spirit. People band together in corporations and partnerships to make economic war on competitors under the rule of law. As long as your company is united against other organizations while maintaining constructive internal competition, you are all right. But a company divided against itself has no future.

Chapter Eleven

# OFFICE MARRIAGE

In business, the process of putting together a work team--regardless of its members' sex--is similar to arranging a marriage. There must be cooperation, mutual respect and concern, anticipation of other's needs, and clear communication. As in a marriage, this business coupling creates a bond through long hours spent together, a sharing of events and information, the making of joint decisions, and defense against criticism. If the team members are of opposite sexes, it is a simple--and obvious--step for such working partners to find themselves acting as though they were wed. They are playing OFFICE MARRIAGE, a game that is always sexual in fantasy even if the partners stop short of overt sex.

## Acting out a hopeless love

Almost anyone in an office setting is susceptible to OFFICE MARRIAGE:

most vulnerable are those trapped in unhappy marriages and singles, especially those with little experience in love. Often played by people who have problems with closeness and trust, the game is bittersweet--based on closeness without fruition. Knowledgeable players may see themselves as acting out the hopeless love of Rick (Humphrey Bogart) and Elsa (Ingrid Bergman) in Casablanca, the legendary World War II movie. She's married to a hero; he's an adventurer; both are caught up in the war, though the encounter is in an exotic locale outside the war zone. They must love while they can, then part--romance without commitment. Even though both parties know it must end, they also realize that they will suffer for their love.

## A romantic duo

A pair of players resemble any happy couple. They spend as much time together as possible, hold hands, nuzzle, kiss, have long, private, intimate conversations, write notes to each other, and trade presents. When one is away on a trip and the other is in the office, they stay in touch by telephone.

## How the couple costs your business

Most of the time, the game can make for a highly productive working team. At other times, the costs may run up--as follows:

• The couple is more loyal to each other than to the company. Apart from the time lost to work in billing and cooing, this can result in conflicts of interest that get resolved to the couple's benefit but work against the interest of the organization.

• The couple can become a closed circle, excluding influences and information from the outside. They may also be unable or unwilling to add others to their team for tasks larger than those that can be accomplished by just two people.

• Their intimacy can arouse the jealousy of other managers and employees and cause loss of morale. The reaction may lead to efforts to sabotage the relationship with rumors, gossip, and negative actions, such as informing the spouses.

## The strength of the dyad

By and large, players who have formed an OFFICE MARRIAGE are as good--or bad--at their work as they were before the union. Once united, they make an inseparable team, or dyad. As such, they may well become increasingly effective in their work habits, since they draw strength from each other. But whether they are effective or not depends on how management handles them. For example, the dyad will resist furiously any attempt to tear it asunder, even if the attempted breach is for the company's--or even their own--benefit. Threatened with separation, they may seek a joint transfer to another division or even talk about quitting. Thus, their indivisibility can be a problem, no matter how skilled they are. Conversely, they work together so well that any task requiring a dedicated couple will be done excellently by them.

## Their relationship is paramount

The players mesh with anyone who doesn't mess with them. They want only to be left alone to enjoy one another. They shun those who are offended, irritated, or critical of their relationship. They are particularly antagonistic to people who are jealous of them.

## Delicate treatment

Solving the problems created for your organization by an OFFICE MAR-
RIAGE requires all the delicacy that you as a boss can muster. The trouble
is that by the time you notice the game in progress, it's usually too late.
Preventing it before it starts is the prime solution. Yet, since anyone is
liable to this game, prevention is difficult. Offices are full of compatible people. Trying to anticipate who will pair off with whom takes a
keen awareness of your personnel.

If possible, limit the frequency and duration of the times that two
people work together on mixed-sex teams. By shifting the composition of
the work teams regularly, you lessen the chance of romantic bonds forming.

Once started, OFFICE MARRIAGE must be allowed to run its course. Step
in to stop it only if it really interferes with the efficiency of the company.

## Admit the marriage exists

Face up to the reality of the dyad. Don't try to ignore it or encourage
your employees to pretend it doesn't exist.

## Should a boss play?

Inasmuch as the best solution to this game is prevention, you as boss
must be particularly leery of falling into an OFFICE MARRIAGE. It is entirely inappropriate for a boss to have a romantic relationship with an employee.

As in the case of SEXUAL HARASSMENT (page 41), once the game is started, the party who is most hurt is the subordinate. If the boss thinks through what he is doing, he must question how much he really cares for the other person.

## The romantic repeater

Most romantics play this game at least once in their work lives with varying outcomes. Hard-core, or third-degree, players form this kind of alliance repetitively; they may never sustain a real relationship outside such office liaisons.

A hard-core player has usually grown up in a difficult family setting, marked by constant marital strife. The experience has weakened belief in the solidity of a personal relationship. The adult substitutes a belief in romance for the values of a lasting union. All a player wants from a relationship is the honeymoon phase--whatever the ultimate costs to the partner. The last thing a player seeks is problems; belief in solutions is lacking because of a sense of inadequacy in the forming of permanent relationships. Such an individual has abandoned the search for a settled relationship--he samples the first squeezings of the grape and then throws away the rest.

## A deep personal problem

They aren't treatable by typical business-world methods such as consultations, workshops, reading, and mentorship. The game reveals a deep personal problem that reflects on business performance. The best hope for a hard-core player is to seek the help of a psychotherapist.

## Advantages of the union

The players of OFFICE MARRIAGE are devoted, energetic workers. Because they want to be together, they come to work every day and absenteeism is low. Their productivity falls off only if they are allowed to spend too much time together lovemaking and romancing. With proper, minimal supervision, they can be at least as good if not better workers than before they got together. Their morale is high and if they are discreet, they don't create problems through such things as jealousies or office gossip.

When the partnership dissolves, assist the players by reassigning them as far from each other as possible within the operation. If your company has branch offices, try to send one of the players to a branch. If the organization is small with all employees in close daily contact, one of the players usually has to leave. If the players have an unusual amount of maturity and sophistication, they might be able to work together in the same office or factory--but if their busted romance disrupts organizational morale, then one must certainly be asked to go.

## When marrieds play

OFFICE MARRIAGE is often played between two people already married, but not to each other. If the game becomes sexual, it can destroy the existing marriages. A subsequent marriage between the two players confirms the American notion that there's an ideal mate out there for everyone, someone to provide sex, partnership, and mutual interest. This desire for the positive outweighs the sorrow for the dislocation of the previous marriage and breakup of families.

## A tempting game

Love springs eternal, especially if not already present. It is impossible not to be tempted by this game, and many working-age males and females are not involved in a satisfactory love relationship. Thus, a majority of the population is ripe for the game.

Attempt to prevent OFFICE MARRIAGE if you can; contiguity in business offices fosters it. It's a frequent phenomenon, and it tends to be a low-key problem. Treating the game with tact, discretion, and understanding may be the best that management can do.

CHAPTER TWELVE

# RAW POWER

The conduct of any business usually implies the exercise of power--in making decisions concerning market expansion and cutbacks, hiring and firing, setting goals, and making plans for the future. The game of RAW POWER spills out beyond the bounds of these normal functions. It is the use of power outside legitimate channels to satisfy the desires of a determined person or institution.

The game has two recognized aspects:

1. External: When someone outside the organization employs illegitimate--or suspect--means to seize control of the company. Often the motivations are predatory, vengeful, or speculative. The procedure, however, entails the manipulation of legitimate institutional power for selfish purposes.

Example: An investment corporation, noticing that the stock of a viable company is unexpectedly low, buys in at bargain rates. Through manipulations, it quietly seizes control of the company. Although the firm has a presence in the community, manufactures a wanted product, and has dedicated employees, managers, and stockholders, the investment corporation sees a chance to make a killing by selling off the productive assets and liquidating the inventory. In the process, the investors quickly turn over more money than the small amount they paid out for undervalued shares on the market. A profitable company has thus been cannibalized for a fast buck by a corporation playing RAW POWER.

2. Internal: The player is hired as a manager or employee, but his lust for command is uncontrollable. When his opportunity arises, he grabs the power in the company and takes over. Usually, the desk he occupies is yours.

## Motivations of outside players

External power grabbers are like sharks. They attack living things, eat all they can, then leave the carcasses floating in the water. What drives these sharks?

• Revenge. It is not uncommon for corporations that have been hurt in the marketplace by competitors to strike back through RAW POWER. Sometimes, the attacks are motivated by personal animosities--the head of one firm wants to get even with his counterpart in another business. Just as lending institutions, such as banks, have been known to grant loans as favors to preferred businessmen, they can also attempt to take control of businesses from those against whom they harbor a grudge.

• Protection. The head of a corporation might use his RAW POWER to maintain the status quo in another, smaller company that he controls. He does this to protect a relative or friend in a high-paying job. Alternatively, he may fear an uprising against him if more vigorous executives take over.

• Short-term venality. Some companies make it a practice to grab vulnerable organizations and sell them off piecemeal for a profit.

## A yearning for kingship

Players within your company are usually highly energetic, aggressive entrepreneurs who work hard but harbor a consuming desire to be king. They make themselves known by continually implying that they could run things better than anyone else.

In managerial positions, these players tend to be tyrannical and are close only with assistants who toady to them. Their slogan is, "Don't get mad, get even."

They are constantly watching for their chance to take over. Here's a cardinal sign: A player, appointed acting supervisor when his boss is out of town, will take permanent actions, such as firing a key aide or altering a vital element of procedure. If this happens, you can be sure you have a dedicated player on your hands.

## The ultimate price

While they are ambitious people who are very productive, these players can be costly since they strike at moments of vulnerability. All they care about is their own power; therefore they must grab it when they can--regardless of how the maneuver affects the business.

Example: During an attempted takeover of your company, a player may be serving as an internal contact for the outside group of speculators. He feeds them information and strategy in return for a promise of a powerful job when the new management prevails.

Of course, the ultimate cost inflicted on you by this player is the deadly one--he grabs your job, your company, or both.


## The key is tight control

You must walk a high wire for these players; you want their energy and skills but you can't allow their ambitions to wreck your company and destroy them as workers. Therefore, maintain tight control over the player and never let your company become vulnerable. The player needs the freedom to operate, yet lines of communication must always be open between you and him.

Watch this player as though he were a thief in your treasury. Make sure you always know what he's doing and why. Don't present him with long periods of unsupervised time--he'll abuse the privilege. Also check regularly with his subordinates as to what he's doing. They will be a willing source of information once they realize your interest.


## Approval by default

The most aggressive players of RAW POWER might have grown up in families in which they were too smart, ambitious, and hard-headed to be controlled by their parents. From an early age, these players simply ran the show. They did whatever they wanted and their parents approved by reason of default.

## Treatment is problematic

Rarely does someone who is so fascinated by command as these players
are willingly grant power to another, such as a consultant or therapist.
Only those players sensitive enough to realize the advantages of becoming
civilized about their power needs are reachable. And then, this suscepti-
bility is initiated by some business or personal disaster or by the mellow-
ing process of aging.

Part Two

# PESSIMISTIC RISK GAMES

The most dangerous games discussed in this book fall into this set. While each of these games is antisocial, two of them--SNOOPER and WORK THE MAN--can be tolerated when kept in their mildest forms. But in general, the players of this quartet often have serious personality disorders; they should be approached by the manager with the utmost caution. At their worst, the players can be destructive and even violent.

# CHAPTER THIRTEEN

# ARE YOU OUT TO GET ME?

Office workers often joke about being paranoid; when asked to perform an unpleasant task or work on an occasional weekend, they might make a quip about the boss being out to get them. But occasionally you will come across an employee who is playing a really paranoid game, the most dangerous one discussed in this book.

The paranoid player is vicious, a person who believes that he must always get the best of others before they get the best of him. The sharpest players are so deceitful that they can overcome the suspicions of even the most reluctant employer. Once installed in the corporation , they advance through connivance, deception, and, if necessary, blackmail. They are hard workers, talented, often charming. But they possess a ruthlessness that is not understood until it is too late by their victims, who unlike them are fairminded.

## Negative and aggressive

The paranoid player is not to be confused with the office grumbler, a depressed person who worries about everybody and everything. The office grumbler is passive, while the paranoid player is aggressive in pursuing his negative aims.

A distinction must also be made between this player and a true paranoid--i.e., a psychotic. Psychotics are the victims of serious mental disease, while a paranoid player learns his behavior through life experience. A typical true paranoid-psychotic is an isolated person who lives in his own fantasy world surrounded by imaginary persecutors. But the player of ARE YOU OUT TO GET ME? has a severe character disorder that employs active paranoid defenses.


## Interviewing the interviewer

When applying for a job, the paranoid player will interview the interviewer. His questions reflect his own conviction that bosses are lying in wait for him.

"How quickly does the boss fire people?" is a question that the player may ask, in one form or another during the interview. The implication here is that employees of the company are customarily fired for little or no reason. The player is therefore certain that if he comes on board he will meet the same fate as the others.

If he is being interviewed for a position with a young company, the paranoid player will question such things as the president's ability to meet the payroll. His manner shows that he believes the company isn't long for this world.

## Questioning trustworthiness

You know you are interviewing a paranoid player when he persists in asking about the trustworthiness of his future fellow workers. His questions project his opinion that they will be untrustworthy and difficult to deal with.

Ask any job applicant how many lawsuits he is currently involved in. If he is mixed up in more than two, you can be pretty sure you're talking to a paranoid player. Litigation represents a breakdown of the social fabric-- most of us try very hard to stay out of court. If the interviewee cannot find alternatives to lawsuits, it indicates he has a serious problem in coming to terms with society. If he is suing the dry cleaner, Sears, his car mechanic, his mother-in-law, and his ex-wife, he's telling you in no uncertain terms that he's playing ARE YOU OUT TO GET ME?

## Review the job record

A review of the applicant's previous job record reveals signs of the player. If an apparently skilled or talented employee has never held a job for more than a year or two--if his record shows frequent job shifts, sometimes after only a few months--he may well be a paranoid player. He may attempt to rationalize his spotty record with explanations that make sense on the surface: "They laid me off during the recession that year," or "My husband is sick often and I have to stay home to take care of him." Or, "I liked the job, but you know how some people are." To this last remark you might well ask, "No, how are some people?" Don't be surprised if the answer is that "some people" are out to get the applicant--and always have been.

Players are often overqualified for the jobs they are seeking. They settle for lesser positions in the hope of being hired in spite of their endless job-hopping. They often succeed because they are accomplished liars who can make you believe what they say, even though they never vary from their fervent inner belief that their fellow workers, including you, the boss, are out to get them.

## What to look for in the office

Employees who play the paranoid game often reveal themselves through exaggerated putdowns of others, and a tendency to interpret events in a negative way. "George could have helped me on this job. Instead, he deliberately took his break at the exact moment I needed him most. It's typical of how he treats me, and his friends aren't much better. I know they're all trying to make me look bad."

You may think you're tough-minded about people, but the paranoid player will always go you one better--or worse. For instance, you might speculate that an employee with a record of absenteeism must have a second job, which accounts for his absences. But his immediate superior, a paranoid player, assures you that the employee in question is an alcoholic. The manager also has every reason to believe, he says, that the employee is the neighborhood flasher everyone has been trying to identify. Suddenly, the paranoid player has made a bizarre leap; an employee guilty of nothing more than absenteeism is transformed into an alcoholic and an offender against public morals.

## Warping your views

The paranoid player's grossly negative portraits of fellow workers

96

may be far from your experience with them. Yet the player can be so convincing that he can warp your own thinking.

A number of organizations have been wrecked by paranoid deputies who isolated the boss from his managers, then fed him all sorts of falsehoods and distortions about his underlings. They can create enormous tempests at work, fomenting crisis after crisis, manufacturing the chaos they thrive on. While others are in turmoil defending themselves or rooting out falsely accused enemies, the paranoid player rules supreme.

## Throwing up roadblocks

The player's paranoid defensive maneuvers erect obstacles to the normal functioning of business. Anyone associated with him must push past his defenses in order to accomplish anything; energy is wasted, time is lost, and work suffers.

The costs increase if a paranoid player is in a supervisory position. People working with him become demoralized and inefficient.

The paranoid manager spends company money for extensive security systems--bugs for overhearing his enemies, tape recording systems to preserve evidence of plotting, and other provocative and expensive means of surveillance.

## Destroying good workers

The paranoid manager may set out to destroy truly competent employees because they represent a direct threat to him. This attack is often successful unless the victims save themselves by resigning, which means you may pay the cost of losing your best workers. The process may lead to the rapid and complete bureaucratization of a zombie-like army of surviving employees who go along with every whim of the paranoid manager.

As he moves up, he costs the company more and more, committing company resources to the construction of barriers against his imaginary enemies.

## Avoid these players

Though he may be intelligent and even talented, the paranoid player is to be avoided at all costs. Paranoid players are a threat in any job. They are not to be hired and if discovered they must be removed as safely and expeditiously as possible. (How to fire one, page 99).

Luckily, there aren't many paranoid players. They make such an impact, however, that even one of them in your business has the destructive effect of an invading army. You may think you can manage him, but you can't. Sooner or later he will set out to destroy you--driven by the paranoid feeling that you, like everyone else, are out to get him.

## Consuming their friends

Though they tend to get along with other paranoid players, they consume their friends, and sooner or later only one player remains.

They also cultivate friendships with mediocrities who pose no threat to them and whom they can manipulate. They are compatible with sycophants who are deft at taking advantage of the chaos the paranoid player generates.

## How to handle a player

These individuals should not be involved in an organizational setting. The extremely talented players can be retained on a freelance basis, under contract and isolated from contact with your employees. In this way, you utilize their skills but deny them the opportunity to inflict their destructive tendences on your people.

## How to fire one

Discharging a player is not always easy. It requires your full attention to ease the paranoid out and not risk a lawsuit.

To justify the outright firing of a paranoid player--and to protect yourself from his certain retaliation--carefully record all his observable negative behavior and actions for three to six months. Then if his dismissal goes to arbitration or litigation, you have the needed documentation to blunt the player's counterattack. Usually, the paranoid backs down when faced with documentation. He doesn't like to lose and he can always find another company to prey upon.

If he shows no sign of caving in, and if you have the grounds, take criminal action and prosecute. Tell him, in effect, "Leave us or we will lock you up."

This may seem an extreme step--and it is. But many paranoid players only respond to the gun-at-the-temple technique. When faced with a court case or time in jail, even the hardest-nosed players will sit up and take notice.

The player will usually leave, sometimes without compensation, to be free of the onus of a trial. If compensation is justified, be fair but not overly generous. Generosity is wasted on a player of this game--his view of humanity is too warped to appreciate kind motives.

## How paranoid players get that way

Hard-core players are the products of severe and grotesque child-rearing practices that often include physical and sexual abuse. As children they were attacked, burned, tortured, locked in closets, and made to repeat absurd and degrading acts. Some examples:

Periodically, a father took his three children into the woods after midnight and threw a handful of coins into the darkness. He ordered the children to find all the coins before they were allowed to go back into bed. They often spent the night in the woods on their hands and knees. Sometimes they never found the coins. Often they never returned to bed, even though they were expected to be in school the next day. One of the children followed suit and chose to imitate the life of his paranoid-player father as a way to retaliate.

Another father swore he would "make a man" of his six-year-old son. A former boxer, the father donned gloves and laced them on his son's hands, and they sparred. The father pulled no punches on the child. Every day from the age of six until he was 15 the boy was knocked silly. The day of reckoning came when the boy grew strong enough to beat his father. He turned on the man, pummeled him mercilessly, and walked away, never to return home. But the damage had been done--the boy opted to become a paranoid player in his adult life.

Thus do players train succeeding generations. The children grow up under brutal treatment. They wonder: If those dearest to them behave in this manner, what can everyone else be like? Once they become big enough, they make sure they will get theirs, even if it means the destruction of other human beings.

## Is there any treatment for hard-core players?

Some milder cases can fit into certain professional environments, such as the criminal justice system where as guards, policemen, deputies, and even lawyers they are a fitting match for their wards. They are cunning enough to keep one step ahead of the prisoners.

Unless you run a jail, however, keep these players out of your business.

## Paranoid transformation

When thwarted, some apparently stable people alter their personalities, shifting from a benign state into something close to the paranoid. This transformation can occur when the employee loses something he values highly--he is denied a due promotion, has a pet project dropped, or sees a dear friend fired. Instead of slipping into depression (a common consequence in many such cases), he becomes a paranoid player by blaming the "SOB" who caused him the heartache.

While a person may have been a stable employee who was universally admired and a good worker, he is now a dangerous player. If he persists in his game, you must exercise the only solution open to you--fire him.

Chapter Fourteen

# ARSON

The forest ranger became a hero. He detected more fires in his region
than any other member of the state forest service that year. In fact, his
region had more fires than the entire state. They were all small blazes, but
the ranger's alertness had saved vast tracts of woodlands. He received
commendations and citations as well as a promotion.

The high rate of fires in the region made the ranger's superiors suspicious, however. After careful investigation, the department concluded
that the fires had all been set by the ranger who detected them. The hero was
an arsonist.

In business, ARSON is a game played on the figurative--and even on the
literal--level. Most players kindle psychological conflagrations, then
arrive miraculously in the nick of time bearing the only available fire ex-
tinguisher.

## Dousing the flames to restore harmony

A psychological fire is any dramatic situation that has the capacity, if unchecked, to harm or destroy the organization or a substantial segment of it. The arsonist works so subtly that his depredations are often unnoticed. He sets important subordinates to clashing, igniting brushfires between them when teamwork is essential. He then enters as the fireman-hero who supposedly douses the flames and restores harmony.

But the Arsonist actually keeps the disputations smoldering by secretly informing each participant that if each had only struck with greater swiftness and force, each could have won the battle. This sets the stage for the next flareup, which is sure to be more intense than the last. Each subordinate is now convinced that he can win next time by striking boldly and without mercy.

The psychological Arsonist shares many of the same qualities of the real arsonist--his eyes glaze at the sight of danger and he is transported in the presence of trouble. He loves acclaim and rewards. And if these forms of attention cease, or don't come to him, his sense of frustration can lead him to light a torch and set real fires. As the forest ranger discovered, real fires can bring rewards, particularly if the Arsonist discovers them. Wanting attention and gratitude, the player proceeds from fireman to Arsonist.

Example: The shipping department is in turmoil; a crisis manager is needed. One man who applies for the job seems perfect since he has a job history of solving such problems. He's hired and sure enough, that crisis in the department is settled. But soon, new brushfires break out. Employees fight, deadlines aren't met without a superhuman effort that is hard to attain because of low morale. The new manager always appears with some new plan or effort that saves the day--but no permanent cures are found. When the manager pulls off a couple of saves, he is praised by top management. Thereafter he is under careful scrutiny.

Feeling a lack of gratitude, the manager may actually set fire to his shipping area--and discover the blaze himself.

## Background and intuition

In sizing up a job applicant, be alert for a previous history of psychological fire-setting in which he is called on to settle recurring turmoil in his area. If his record shows crisis after crisis, ask yourself, "If he's so good at settling difficult situations, why is he forever in the middle of them?"

Don't ignore your intuition. If a voice inside your head is saying, "I'm worried about this guy even though he looks good right now," then don't hire him.

## Economic and psychological damages

The employment of an Arsonist is an expensive course. Here are just some of the penalties:

• Products, time, and efficiency lost during the unnecessary crises provoked by the Arsonist.

• The distraction of mobilizing people and energy to solve the crisis.

• The price of rewarding the Arsonist who, if encouraged, will repeat his disruptive deeds.

104

• Spreading demoralization and fear among personnel affected by the fires, whose mysterious recurrence is disheartening.

This game can be played with money as a substitute for fire. Here's how it works and what it costs:

A manager torments his employees at intervals by announcing that his cash flow is insufficient to meet the payroll. Yet at the last moment on Friday, he miraculously produces the money. His workers go home shaking, sweating, and wondering how they would have managed over the weekend. The boss sets fire to his employees emotionally, then douses them with water to save them. Talented workers with other job options won't continue to work for that boss very long.

## The few remedies

A crucial preventative is to refrain from rewarding people excessively for putting out fires in crises. Such payoffs by the boss may encourage an employee who's a latent Arsonist, and is feeling disaffected and bitter, to say to himself, "So that's how you win at this game." Unwittingly, the boss creates an Arsonist out of a marginal player. Rewards for helping overcome crises should be limited and certainly not exaggerated.

If the Arsonist is an accomplished worker who is valuable to the company, it may be worth your while to help him start psychotherapy. Your support and understanding could help a player shake off his game and remain a productive worker.

Encourage colleagues to be tolerant of an Arsonist who is seeking professional help. However, those players who continuously create crises to get attention should be denied any organizational support.

## Arson in the executive suite

It is quite possible for the game to be played by the top manager.

Example: The boss invariably makes poor personnel selections--he is constantly hiring dummies who set fires to hide their incompetence. The pattern is: An incompetent and poorly motivated manager is hired for a position of responsibility in which he predictably fails. The boss must then rush in and save the day. But instead of taking on more qualified help, he again hires a bumbler who repeats the pattern. This form of brushfires and extinguishings is expensive and disruptive. The costs to the business and its employees are incalculable.

Any boss who suspects he might be playing this game should examine his behavior from two points of view:

1. Are you in business to make money? Or do you prefer to make trouble, then be the rescuing hero? Being a hero to your victims is an expensive, tedious, destructive process. You need to reevaluate whether your business is an appropriate place to derive that kind of excitement.

2. Usually, covert excitement and approval-seeking is based on a lot of turmoil in childhood. If you see yourself doing this, it's a signal to seek professional help in working through whatever personality problems the behavior may be expressing.

## The thrill of playing with matches

An Arsonist who exhibits severe behavior patterns usually has a childhood history of getting siblings or fellow students in trouble. He might also have been able to set one parent against the other. Often the child was an actual fire-setter. He enjoyed the thrill of lighting the

matches and the excitement of watching people discover the blaze and firemen putting it out. He may even turn in the alarm himself. Then he can wit-
ness the crowds, the arrival of the firemen and police all ready to participate in his spectacular production.

These extreme players are emotionally isolated from other people.
Often they lack good peer relationships. Although they establish a veneer
of socialization as they mature, the internal child remains--the one still
interested in the activity that surrounds fires.

These players represent one of the most intransigent personal patho-
logies. Arsonists who set real fires usually require institutionalization. But most institutions have little or no therapeutic capacity for
curing the game and the players often pass into the category of hopeless
cases. At certain therapeutic communities, however, the players may learn
new ways to reshape their behavior to win the approval they previously received for arson behavior.

In any case, for these players, on-the-job solutions are not adequate.

# Chapter Fifteen

# SNOOPER

A Snooper must know everything that's going on, especially if it's none of his business. He moves from desk to desk, work station to work station, collecting information as a bee flits from flower to flower gathering pollen. While visiting, a Snooper determines what each worker is doing, makes remarks to stimulate the exchange of gossip, and listens discreetly to private conversations or phone calls.

He is the town crier in any office or factory, except that he speaks in whispers and his information is seldom 100% accurate. In companies where information is at a premium, however, a Snooper is sometimes the only reliable source.

Only the most advanced, or hard-core, players betray themselves as Snoopers during a prehiring interview. Usually, players don't commit themselves to their game until they have mastered the company's culture, i.e., have gotten to know everyone, what his job is supposed to be, and what people are really up to. This may take years from the time the Snooper is first signed on.

## "Nothing got past him"

Sometimes the only way to find out if a job applicant is playing Snooper is to talk to former colleagues. If in describing him they say, "He had to know what was happening," or, "He was so interested in everyone's private lives," or, "Nothing in the company--private or personal--got past him. He knew more of what was going on than our chairman of the board," then you have a potential Snooper.

On the job, a fully functioning player couldn't be more obvious if he waved a banner emblazoned with the word "Snooper." He talks endlessly about company doings and the latest scandals among his colleagues and bosses. Any sign of interest will spur him on--usually with the request of payment through an exchange of gossip.

A cardinal sign of a Snooper is his genius for being on hand exactly when the utmost secrecy is desired. He appears at a project's most sensitive moment to observe and remember all the vital details--even though he is not connected with the job.

## A well-honed intuition

His keen sense of timing is no accident. Part of the technique of playing Snooper is to be constantly floating around the work areas, which increases the probability of being at the right place at the right time. A player also has a well-honed intuition about things going wrong: emergencies ring a loud alarm bell in his awareness and he directs himself immediately toward the most juicily awkward situations.

A Snooper will also try to rearrange his job assignment to include maximum contact with as many people from different divisions and segments of the business as possible. This helps him toward his need to be in on everything.

Example: A bookkeeper could ask that every department head and section manager send all invoices, vouchers, and other financial paper to his office. Instead, he goes around to each area to collect them. During his rounds of the plant, the bookkeeper makes small talk, most of which is directed toward what everyone is doing at work--and in their spare time. This information, along with what he learns from handling the books, gives the bookkeeper his inside dope. His penchant for leaving his desk to "get to know" his colleagues is really a front for gathering his information.

## A gigantic waste

The main damage caused by the game is the amount of time wasted by the Snooper and his fellow employees. Every bit of gossip or trivia relayed or picked up by the Snooper subtracts from company productivity. Some other negative effects:

• If a Snooper becomes bitter and disloyal, his predilection may turn him into a spy. The costs of having company secrets fed directly to competitors can be staggering.

• Organizations that tolerate Snoopers tend to nurture COVER YOUR TRACKS (page 206) and ARE YOU OUT TO GET ME (page 93); games that decrease productivity and efficiency through concern with defensive maneuvering.

110

• In larger corporations, Snoopers can cause cooperation between divisions to break down through the repetition of half-truths or slanderous gossip. When this happens, the company risks fragmentation as territorial concerns become paramount (see TERRITORY, page 72).

## Plugging leaks

Keep a Snooper out of any part of the firm that depends on discretion or delicate handling of details.

Example: A cosmetics company that creates new formulas for perfumes or essences doesn't need a Snooper in the research lab. He's a natural source of leakage of trade secrets and may in fact end up recruited as a spy for a competitor.

Snoopers are also dangerous during times of company reorganizations and major shakeups as they may prematurely tattle on plans and prospects, which creates serious problems of morale.

• Don't hire Snoopers for work that involves advance planning--they don't make reliable private secretaries or executive assistants. Nor should they be in positions where they deal with governmental agencies-- they tend to tell all.

## The uses of a Snooper

On the positive side, Snoopers make excellent investigators--the role is a perfect match between their game and a necessary kind of job. This professional category would include such jobs as credit investigator, background checker, insurance adjuster, collection agency--and private detective.

Inside an organization that doesn't have these positions, Snoopers do well in researching employment histories, which includes checking references of those wishing to be hired or to do business with the company. Players are also skilled purchasing agents who can sniff out good deals and form useful alliances with dealers based on insider's knowledge.

Snoopers are almost necessary in organizations that have installed one-way communications from the top down. Under this system, the line employees and supervisors seldom have knowledge of advance planning and the managers are in the dark about conditions on the line. This places a premium on accurate information, no matter how it is delivered. Thus the Snooper fills a needed social role by spreading the word informally.

Snoopers love the voluble of any persuasion. Anyone who'll talk, they'll listen; any who'll listen, they'll talk. They are turned off by reserved, private types who regard gossip as a waste of time. Snoopers are also ignored or closed out by people whose moral standards lead them to disdain gossips.

## Neutralizing the player

The way to short-circuit the power of the Snooper is to establish a two-way system of communication, which denies the secrets and sores of resentment that can fester in any company in which workers are kept in the dark.

How to establish a two-way communications system:

• Regularly publish newsletters and memos that are distributed to all employees. These should contain all pertinent nonconfidential information.

• Train and supervise managers so that they hold regular meetings with personnel under their command. These gatherings should be open-ended, a chance for the company to explain its position and for workers to air grievances, discuss problems, make suggestions, share ideas, and receive feedback and evaluation.

• Managers should be encouraged to walk the company floor for brief, informal contacts with employees on a regular basis. If done in an open manner, these meetings provide a relaxed forum for supervisor and worker to discuss matters in an offhand way without the pressures that go with a larger, more formal gathering.

• In small, tightly knit organizations, it sometimes helps to arrange an occasional weekend or day out of the office when employees can discuss planning, problems, ideas, and issues. These times together create casual, face-to-face contacts between managers and the managed (who might be physically separated during most working hours) and generate the free, open exchange of information.

• Give rapid attention to grievances by regularly holding informal hearings to solve problems at the lowest level. This generates the comforting feeling among employees that their troubles will be listened to and dealt with quickly and fairly.

Once two-way communication is firmly entrenched, the Snooper will cease being a powerful negative force in the busines--relegated to a more tolerable role as office gossip.

## Tattletales

Those who play the game in the third degree usually learned it in

childhood through successful tattletaling. They were also often encouraged by squabbling parents who told them intimate details of the fights,
and turned them into more or less malevolent go-betweens carrying messages
back and forth between warring mother and father.

A Snooper also develops his exquisite sense of timing at an early age.
A child who comes home from school in the middle of the day claiming some
vague sickness when one of the parents is conducting an extramarital affair in the bedroom is a born Snooper.

In school, the hard-core Snooper is the one who turns in fellow students for cheating on exams. Or, he will tell the principal that the gym
teacher, Mr. Jones, is secretly meeting after class with Mrs. Smith, the
home economics teacher. At work, the more predatory player will turn to
blackmail, both personal and industrial.

These unpleasant people must not be nourished by the company. Their
prying and slander must be renounced or it will be interpreted as company
policy. A player who can't drop the game or won't seek counseling should be
let go.

Chapter Sixteen

# WORK THE MAN

This is a class-oriented game, played by workers who come from different ethnic, religious, or racial backgrounds than the managers. In the game, the player squeezes every ounce of money, privilege, sympathy, and free time from the boss (The Man), especially one who is sympathetic to the workers--indeed, feels guilty about their situation.

When there is no opportunity for advancement for the workers, the game is widespread. This lack of upward mobility also introduces the elements of a master-slave relationship, marked by a profound lack of understanding between worker and manager.

This relationship fosters the projection of stereotypes: The workers in the underclass tend to view The Man as a moderately benevolent enemy who is fair game. Conversely, managers often regard the workers as downtrodden souls who are worthy of pity, but whose alien ways make them nuisances.

WORK THE MAN is an obvious game, yet it does have its subtleties. Since the workers suffer from various degrees of economic stress, their money needs are real; yet often their game ploys are pure fabrication. The game stands as something of a sport to be bragged about over drinks bought by the player with The Man's money. Ironically, the best players, skillful and shrewd, could make the finest managers.

## An early touch

Players start their game while applying for the job. If you indicate that you may hire them, they will immediately request a salary advance. This will be accompanied by a long story whose point is that you're a hard-hearted SOB if you don't come across. Sometimes the game ends at that stage as the hiree takes the advance, then never shows up for work.

If you yield on the salary advance, the game is established as the player is rewarded for Working The Man. But these players are often the only ones willing to do the unskilled jobs scorned by those who possess some degree of upward mobility. Thus, even if you try to screen out the applicants and hire just those who don't play this game, you will never fill your unskilled labor force. The game is endemic--it comes with workers who are shut off from advancement. The secret for management is learning to recognize and deal with it.

## Cultivating The Man

Those who go out of their way to cultivate The Man in ways that are not appropriate in the work setting are playing the game. Unnervingly persistent, they sidle up to catch the boss at weak moments.

Example: An empty flatbed truck is pulled up to the warehouse platform where a gang of men stand ready to load. One of the workers takes the boss aside to involve him in a long, complex story about an illness in his family requiring special medical treatment, which translates into immediate cash. The boss, kept from the job of loading, finds himself agreeing to pay the money just to rid himself of the annoyance. The player had been willing to hold up the boss for hours in order to get his money.

Striking at times of vulnerability is essential to a successful outcome of the game. The player waits until the manager is up to his neck in work, then he plays on the man's guilt to hit him up for more money or a day off or some special favor.

Some of the guilt derives from the knowledge that the workers are in dead-end positions--they will never earn the salaries or hold the responsibility that management does. This runs counter to the sense of fair play that we are schooled to believe is intrinsic in our society. And, no matter how well treated the workers have been in the recent past, there has been enough mistreatment to plant seeds of guilt. Thus, the consciousness that his job is a dead-end position, with a background of maltreatment of his caste or class or race, gives the player a real edge in the game.

## Neither too hard nor too soft

Remember: players enjoy doing their routines--it provides them with a moment in the spotlight when someone important is listening to them. Even if he doesn't come up with the reward--cash, time off, special favor--the player has had the opportunity to be heard. The boss, therefore, must be patient and sensitive enough to hear out the player. In its best sense, the game is an acceptable form of social interaction between two people who have little in common. The game is best controlled by the manager adopting the classic firm-but-fair stance. He should be neither a slavemaster nor a benevolent sucker.

## Training the manager to accommodate the players

Other workers neither help nor hinder a player while he is performing his game. They stand back without interfering. The best way to accommodate the player, then, is to train his boss to be understanding in the firm-but-fair mode. If the boss has control of the situation, the player does not use his game obsessively, so he isn't fired or banished to tasks that are beneath his skills.

A good manager can weld a disparate group into an efficient work force while an untrained boss can take the same men and end up under their control with little being accomplished. The secret is to be consistent.

Also effective: a humorous confrontation of the player--after hearing him out for a reasonable amount of time. Usually, the game will be dropped, probably with the player saying goodhumoredly, "You can't blame me for trying."

## Agree to play

Accept the fact that it's the right of underclass workers to play WORK THE MAN just as it's the manager's right to refuse to be worked. Once both sides are clear on this point, the problem should recede.

The game allows for the ventilation of a lot of feelings by a player who feels he's a victim of society--without his losing face. While most of his stories portray him as the victim, his aggressive presentation helps him restore or maintain his pride and self-esteem. It also enables him to hold up his head among his peers--he knows how to Work The Man, even if he's only occasionally successful. Instead of being a crybaby who complains to his boss, he becomes a man for trying to win The Man over to his cause. Thus, in its way, the game can help some workers to continue being productive--as long as it is kept in check.

Part III

# OPTIMISTIC SECURITY GAMES

All security games diminish the players who are motivated not by a desire to excel, but to hang back. Those deeply involved fear risks and want only to survive from day to day. Often these people have been hurt badly by life, enough so that they hide from its challenges.

Of these security-minded players, the optimistic are still hunting for a way to accomplish something. Their dilemma arises from their desire to achieve and their craving for the safe. This often leads them into a dependency on authoritarian figures, as in TRUE BELIEVER (page 130) and FATHER KNOWS BEST (page 143).

Chapter Seventeen

# GIVE
# AWAY

Mike is good at his job, but he has an odd handicap: he likes to give things to his fellow workers. He even sets up his colleagues on the coffee line--Danish sweet rolls and cups of coffee all around. Even when the others object, Mike insists, although his generosity leaves him strapped.

## The catch

But Mike isn't just being a good guy. He is trying to buy love and respect through gifts and favors. Indirectly, he's trying to bind his fellow workers to him through his beneficence. Mike is playing GIVE AWAY.

In return for his kindness, Mike expects gratitude. When those he has favored fail to reciprocate, Mike starts to grumble about their ingratitude. By now, the game starts to control Mike's work habits. It can cause real on-the-job problems both for Mike and for his boss.

## A player's quirks

Before he joins your company, a player reveals himself during the job interview in several ways:

- He often bears a gift with which he hopes to ingratiate himself. It could be a journal or a book about your business, or even something as simple as the day's edition of the Wall Street Journal. During the interview he will promise to send you a copy of a book that comes up in conversation--and he will follow through.

- He volunteers his services, or makes undue sacrifices. He might say, "I'll come on board a week early without pay." Or he could insist that he forego his first year's vacation as a sign of his eagerness to please. Similarly, he might be so accommodating as to offer to start working for the company at night while he dutifully completes the 30-day notice at his current job.

Sometimes a player tips his hand even before the interview begins. "Are you sure no one else needs that interview time?" he asks when the interview is being arranged. His intention is to surrender his time as a gift to someone else, in order to make clear from the start that he is an accommodating soul.

## Visible in the office, though

Because they are so anxious to please, players are easy to hire and they make good workers. Often their game isn't seen until they are on the payroll and exhibit these signs:

- The player volunteers to accept less pay in order to help the company through a time of financial stress.

122

- the Giver rarely says "no", even to unreasonable requests. He will accept difficult work shifts and assignments without a murmur, no matter how often he is asked.

## When the pain starts

The game begins to hurt the player and his productivity as the grumbling sets in.

If the player is like Mike, who buys coffee and rolls for his office mates and still isn't allowed into their social circle, he may come to you with his complaints. Or he could vent his dissatisfaction to third parties. If you overhear Mike muttering to someone about the ingratitude of those who shared his gifts but did not reciprocate with love or friendship, then you can bet that you have a player in an advanced stage of the game of GIVE AWAY.

A sure sign is some form of sulking, which usually occurs after multiple runthroughs of the game. The Giver retreats to pout. He won't respond to questions, seals his lips to small talk, and refuses to relate to anyone in the office.

The terminal symptom: the Giver, who has been an exceptional worker with a bright future, suddenly requests transfer--or even quits his job-- for reasons that make no sense. His explanations are of the Mickey Mouse variety: he might say he has to leave the area to be close to his favorite aunt who is ill in another state. Actually, he is escaping the ungrateful ones who took his gifts without an accompanying surge of affection. The Giver seeks more compatible workers in another division of the company or with a different employer.

## An Expensive Breakdown

When a Giver senses that you or your employees are ungrateful for his gifts, he can suffer a breakdown of personality, which can be expensive in various ways:

• The player increases his alcohol consumption, which leads to decreasing efficiency.

• Preoccupation with his grievance generates irresponsibility. "Gee, I guess I forgot to write up that proposal," he admits after it is too late.

• A surly, uncooperative attitude makes meetings unproductive. In general, relationships at work become more and more difficult. The company loses as the player's associates spend increasing amounts of time listening to him bitching and moaning about their ingratitude. A related cost to the company is the decreasing morale of those who must continue to work with him.

• Errors in judgment appear, often at times that appear deliberately arranged by the player. For example, an employee in charge of resolving a difficult contract negotiation misses a key meeting when his car runs out of gas. The player may claim that running out of gas was an accident, but his poor judgment in forgetting to fill the gas tank led to the costly error. The Giver sought vengeance against those he considered ungrateful, and a valuable contract is lost to the company.

## Jobs they fill well

Givers are generous and magnanimous, therefore well suited for jobs that require relating to people--clients, customers, and other employees.

Givers are good in the personnel department, as heads of training programs, and, naturally, as salesmen. They are also fine in number two positions. Their giving natures also make them perfect receptionists,
secretaries, mail room and errand boys.

## They can't say no

Givers find it impossible to say no. Therefore, they shouldn't be
placed in positions where firm bargaining is demanded. Givers shouldn't
represent the company, for instance, in labor relations. Nor should they
face the public in combative positions --such as serving behind a com-
plaint counter.

Givers aren't tough enough to hold fellow workers to a budget. They
will exhaust company reserves rather than deny monetary requests. Thus,
Givers should never be allowed to handle money as accountants or
treasurers.

## They like whoever likes them

Givers live on gratitude, both in action and verbally. Thus, they get
along with other Givers and Gracious Takers (page 34)--those who say thank
you in a convincing way. In short, Givers are compatible with anyone who
reciprocates. By contrast, Givers don't mesh with cold, abrupt, self-
centered Takers.

## How to place givers

On the job, Givers should be matched with compatible personality
types, i.e., either other Givers or gracious Takers. As much as possible,

separate the Givers from the hard-nosed Takers--who will quickly take all the Giver has.

In some cases, Takers have Givers on their staffs, some in jobs for which they are not suited. For instance, a controller who's a hard-nosed Taker may treat his supporting cast of Givers--bookkeepers, accountants,and clerks--like slaves. To prevent the eventually destructive effect of such treatment, establish carefully articulated limits on what the company expects of the controller's staff so that their boss won't push them too hard.

By the same token, don't create demands that will overextend the Givers. They will do almost anything to please, including working long hours, sometimes beyond their endurance. Resist the temptation to submit to their willingness to be exploited.

## Limits on work load

You must provide tight limits on how much work each Giver is assigned. Supply help for him on big jobs and teach him to delegate authority and responsibility. Help the Giver to care for himself and be alert to signs of stress.

Above all, the Giver must be appreciated. Award ample compensation for his overextensions--overtime pay, extra time off, verbal commendation. Never overlook those most obvious times of remembrance--a Christmas bonus and a day off (and gift) on his birthday. All Givers are waiting for Santa Claus; to them, such holidays as Christmas, birthdays, and even Thanksgiving are extremely important. A boss who marks these days in a Giver's life will hardly need to worry.

## Protect the Giver

If a Giver is exploited by his associates, intervene on his behalf. For example, after your salesmen divide up their territories you notice that the Giver has been assigned all the hard-to-sell clients or those with the smallest accounts. He has no doubt volunteered to take all the hard cases as a gift to his fellow salesmen. Don't let them get away with it: step in and redraw the territories for a more equitable distribution. The principle of fairness applies doubly to a Giver because he is often so unfair to himself.

## Are you a Giver?

Ask yourself these questions: Why am I giving this? What do I expect in return? Is it a reasonable expectation? What will I do if others don't reciprocate?

If, when answering these questions, you find yourself becoming angry at someone who hasn't returned a favor you did for him, you're probably playing the game.

If you realize that you're a Giver, yet you still want to present the gift, draw up a memorandum setting out the specific payback you'll expect to receive. Let's say you grant an employee a special leave to tend to some family business, even though his absence will interfere with the completion of a vital project. You must set out a procedure for the employee to repay you for this time off--with a written promise to work overtime to put the project back on schedule.

Don't make the common mistake of simply assuming that on his return the employee will work hard to complete the project. He may not appreciate its importance as much as you do.

## Anatomy of a chronic player

The dynamics of the game are shown in their most extreme and dramatic form by hard-core players. This type of Giver will offer goods, money, favors, time, and energy on minimal acquaintance. If you accept his offerings, more soon follows. This chronic Giver is hard to resist since he is keen at spotting your needs.

When the player was a youth, at least one parent (or parent figure) was ungiving. The Giver tried everything he could to gain the favor of the unyielding parent. Occasionally, he was successful and the parent would respond in a favorable way. This encouraged the Giver to try even harder. In the end, however, the unyielding parent did not reciprocate, and the Giver was left frustrated and angry.

From this experience, the Giver nurtured a belief that if he could just grow big enough to give sufficiently good gifts, he'd be able to convince people to respond with the love, gratitude, affection, and trust that he lacked as a child. Having noted at an early age the power of gifts and favors to bind some people at least temporarily, he now wants to tie others to him permanently by means of the more extensive generosity available to an adult.

In reality, however, his adult experiences are close to those of his childhood. The Giver's gifts are likely to meet with a rebuff--just as when offered to the unyielding parent.


## Programs that help

The inevitable answer for the third-degree Giver is psychotherapy, which may take from one to three years. Adjuncts that are easily available include assertiveness training, such as EST, Dale Carnegie, and other achievement-oriented self-help programs.

You can assist this Giver by drawing up contracts that clearly define his job limits. This will keep him from falling into the trap of pushing himself so hard that he becomes ill from trying to please. (Also, arrange for similar agreements with your other employees, and make sure that they are fair.) If you take it upon yourself to watch out for this dedicated player, you will retain a willing, loyal employee.

## A game that claims no fatalities

Even the most extreme players of GIVE AWAY can be changed for the better with such specific programs as those outlined above. Nobody dies from this game. On the contrary, with growing maturity and the aid of contracts, most players live long, productive, happy working lives.

Mild though it may be, however, you and your employees must face up to the game and set about eliminating or lessening its effects. The alternative may be a growing isolation and bitterness on the part of the player, who is an otherwise valuable worker.

Chapter Eighteen

# TRUE BELIEVER

The player is someone convinced he has found The Truth. The exact nature of this Truth varies with the player: on the spiritual side, a True Believer may suddenly find God or a special means of understanding and appreciating the Nature of the Universe; on the material side, he can invest his belief in a new business technique or sales approach.

No matter what the belief, True Believers find it insufficient merely to possess The Truth. Their deep insecurities drive them to sell this Truth; this proves that they actually have it.

Most of us have some of the True Believer in us. It is part of our longing for faith and a striving for perfection in our lives. Yet the game of TRUE BELIEVER exceeds these typical feelings. It carries within it a passion for the crusade, a need to convert others, and a willingness to employ a cause to vault higher in the social order.

## A natural home in business

All these drives are familiar in business, where the True Believer finds a natural niche. Indeed, many businesses and entire corporations have been structured around the uses of True Belivers.

For example, certain companies sell their products through local representatives. While the products may be worthy, the success of the business depends on a small army of True Believers who swarm across the marketplace selling to their friends, their neighbors, and total strangers. Nor is this selling haphazard; it is structured through distribution pyramids.

Here's how it works: One person signs on as a salesperson. He recruits other salespeople who are responsible to him. The original salesperson then draws a commission from whatever his recruits sell--as well as the straight commission from what he sells himself. The recruits then bring new salespeople into the structure from whom they in turn take commissions. Soon the base of the pyramid broadens with the original salesperson at the top drawing commissions from those below him.

Everything from home products to cosmetics is sold in this fashion by companies that are nationally known--Amway, Mary Kay Cosmetics. Yet the product doesn't really matter--the sales structure is entirely dependent on True Believers. They must be convinced that they have found a Truth, which they must sell to others who then become their recruits.

## Using a religious approach

The techniques used by these businesses to attract True Believers resemble those employed at revival meetings. There are songs about the product, spiels by successful people who have profited from life atop the sales pyramid, and there is usually a charismatic founder who appears at the climactic moment amid a shower of lights and swelling music to place his benediction on the enterprise.

While TRUE BELIEVER extends to both sexes, bored housewives are most often recruited for these sales schemes. They are given an opportunity to leave the routine of housework and lose themselves in a noble cause--one that can make them rich.

## True belief and your company

The game is intrinsic to the founding of any business, particularly one with an entrepreneurial tone. Young businessmen are often headed by a charismatic founder who excites the loyalty of workers and lures top talent from competitors with his passionate sermons about the glowing future of the enterprise. They will all grow strong, powerful, and wealthy together. This dynamic pitch appeals to the True Believer in most of us. And those willing to forego their cautions are swept away by the boss's enthusiasm. True Believers are willing to work long hours under difficult conditions for lower-than-average pay to help a fledgling company test its wings. They want nothing more than a chance to buy into the dream.

## Roots in childhood

TRUE BELIEVER takes hold only in a susceptible person and then only after a vigorous, hard sell. The game is rooted in the childhood of the player. All children strive to master their universe. Many parents, however, close the child's mind. They encourage him to believe that the

parents have already discovered the correct working model of the universe.
As the child grows into adolescence, he rejects the parents' model of
belief. But he doesn't turn away from belief as such. He is actually seeking
a substitute belief for his parents' model; he is a prime candidate to
become a True Believer.

Although the True Believer is always highly susceptible to being
taken over, his mode is to fight it. He wants to be convinced by a person
dynamic enough to overcome his feigned reservations. Part of the game is a
denial by the player that he is playing it; then when a leader or cause appears that is strong enough to override these objections, the player suc-
cumbs while telling himself that he didn't want to play but couldn't
resist.


## Zealous converts

Players, particularly in their early phase of conviction, bubble
over with unsolicited comment on the powers of their newly found solutions
to old problems--or on the excitement of being involved with a new boss or
company that is going places. They repeat blindly the cliches of the project: "A chance to get in on the ground floor," if they are associated with a
new business. Or, if buying a franchise manipulated by a high-powered entrepreneur, "This is a chance to get into business for myself."

Their language, looks, and attitudes radiate their conviction. They
may rush up to strangers ready to impart The Word. They want everyone to
share their excitement, and if they are selling a product they will shame-
lessly try to enlist buyers--or recruits as salespeople--on the spot.
Their pitch is a version of: "It's so simple to make money. Just follow my

lead and do what I do. I know it will work. I have it on the highest authority."

## When belief sags

At first blush, this game seems cost-free from the company's viewpoint. Yet it doesn't always work out that way. True Believers can become disillusioned almost as quickly as they were converted. When their belief lags, so does their performance. This means that a Believer whose fires are banked is not half the worker--or salesperson--he once was.

Basically, True Believers are unsure of themselves. They need constant reassurance to relieve those tuggings of inadequacy. Not every company or every charismatic leader can provide this constant attention. Therefore, there is a high turnover rate among Believers.

## Searching for a system of beliefs

Most people who grew up in a family that emphasized believing in something will emerge from childhood believing in belief. The person who plays TRUE BELIEVER in its most extreme form is committed to an absolute belief. Yet, while always passionate, his beliefs are not always durable--they may change from time to time.

The heart of the problem for this player is that no system of belief is an accurate model of reality under all circumstances. The discrepancies between the real world and the player's current model of reality are both painful and costly to him. The player spends a lot of time and energy justifying his current belief in relation to the model of reality.

It is this disparity between the player's model and the Real World that lends the game its fascinating complexities. I believe there is a Real World. Not everyone does. My favorite definition of reality is "consensually validated illusion." This is just a fancy way of saying that we humans tend to see what we believe we see. The belief is only partly based on incoming stimuli: we tend to see what we want to see, or what we've been told to see, or what we've previously seen. We don't always see what is actually there.

When humans were told that the earth was flat, they saw it as such and believed it. Similarly, men were convinced that the earth was the center of the universe. All the best minds assured them this was so and their daily perceptions confirmed it--people saw what they were ready to believe. When proof was offered that the earth was not flat (and not the center of the universe), many humans fought to preserve their previously held beliefs. They could not assimilate the new, unfamiliar facts into their model of reality.

Such an inflexibly held view enables the player to match his perceived model of reality with the real world. But the fact is basically wrong. Thus, at bottom, the committed True Believer has only his zeal to make it work. His deep sense of personal inadequacy further fuels his enthusiasm for evangelizing. By insisting that others conform to his sense of mission, the player may win converts. But he also denies his true ability to appreciate the real world--and his place in it.

Unless your business is set up to accommodate--or exploit--these evangelical players, their zeal can be counterproductive. It decreases the efficiency of the player and those who are subjected to his evangelical assaults.

## Breaking up the game

Players face two basic choices:

1. The player can accept his True Belief as his way of life. He might join a stable community of other True Believers and settle down. With this part of the game worked out, the player can often lead a productive life.

2. Many players must deal with the basic psychological issues pertinent to their game. Through maturation and psychotherapy they learn to identify and deal with the insecurities they brought with them from childhood. Through this new awareness and their own belief in themselves, they will start to feel better about themselves. Then the need for true believing will slip away.

The world's population is largely made up of True Believers and most of them are good workers. Those who are advocates of old-line, conservative true beliefs tend not to proselytize, particularly on the job. Evangelical True Believers, however, can disrupt work and become real nuisances.

True belief should be used positively as an affirmation of self. Forbid evangelical preaching on the job--it is only the broadcasting of the player's deep insecurities.

Chapter Nineteen

# GOODY
# TWO-SHOES

A Goody Two-Shoes lives to please. He will say or do almost anything to accommodate a fellow human being, particularly one vested with any type of authority. If his game goes unchecked, the Goody runs the risk of turning into a smiling automaton, a soul bereft of the power to contribute creatively.

Ironically, the problems of a Goody are also his virtues. Punctual, seldom absent, meticulous, and a glutton for extra work, he builds a good record and wins the heart of the boss. Yet he only performs well when he is told exactly what to do. When his diligence leads to his promotion to a responsible position, the Goody usually fails. Instead of taking charge, he aims his desire to please toward those working under him. He starts doing what his underlings tell him just so that they won't be mad at him. At the same time, the Goody is trying to placate management by abiding by its desires. Instead of leading, the Goody is ground between the demands of his superiors and the gripes of his workers.

Thus does the Goody embody the Peter Principle. He is an excellent worker who boasts an admirable record and years of seniority; placed in a job beyond his capabilities, his game destroys his effectiveness.

## A bad bargain for the player

Since this game is a version of GIVE AWAY (page 121), the player announces his role early, as does a Giver. But while Givers seek reciprocity from those to whom they give, the Goody expects nothing. He wants only not to be hurt or rejected. While a Giver has a limit to his beneficence, a Goody will keep on giving indefinitely.

The Goody will attempt to adapt from the very first phone call to arrange the job interview. He'll bend every effort to learn what your company expects of him by asking such questions as, "What do you want me to wear?" Or, "Do you allow smoking during the interview? I smoke an occasional cigarette, but I'll be glad to give it up."

In conversation, the Goody will refuse to say the word no. He will also be agreeable to almost any condition of employment, even those that may embarrass the interviewer because of their natural disadvantage for the Goody. Some examples:

• The interviewer might make an absurdly low salary offer, just as a basis for negotiation, then he is astounded when the Goody answers, "If that's what you think I'm worth, it's good enough for me."

• The interviewer may place a demanding condition on the job. He wants the player to travel to a new city and report to work that same day without even a chance to unpack or become acclimated. The Goody won't blink but will respond with a hearty, "Yes sir."

## Low-keyed and inconspicuous

The player avoids the aggressions of others by not attracting attention to himself or offering a point of resistance. He will dress in whatever style is low-keyed and current--anything that permits him to fade into the background. He avoids loud colors and flamboyant styles.

A Goody smiles constantly and even tends to simper. He's the one who always ends up running errands--he either volunteers or is selected for his apparent willingness.

A player can occupy an uncomfortable work slot that would have driven a more aggressive or well-rounded employee screaming from the office. Often such a position is occupied by a female Goody who works as an assistant or secretary to a tyrannical manager. She is usually referred to this way: "She's a saint to be able to abide that monster for all these years."

## Dead ends

In the short run, a Goody contributes to the company by his eagerness and devotion to work. In the long run, however, his inability to handle responsibility signifies a limit on both his function and his usefulness to the company.

In day-to-day matters, a Goody limits himself by following stupid orders blindly. Or he can make a manager look bad--and cost the company money--by withholding vital information for fear of upsetting a superior. This is a classic problem in a large business or bureaucracy.

Example: A Goody, who thoroughly knows the machine he operates, is told to run it at a rate above its safe capacity. The Goody raises a mild objection by saying that the machine needs certain repairs. When the supervisor pays no attention and tells the Goody to run the machine all-out, he doesn't protest. He follows orders--and allows an expensive machine to tear itself to shreds.

The Goody feels he acted properly in warning the supervisor about the problems, but he should have refused point-blank to ruin the machine--he knew its state better than anyone, including the supervisor.

These players are excellent at tasks that require a minimum of creativity or initiative. This is as true at the professional level as on the assembly line: A Goody lawyer is better at preparing contracts or at research than he is at independent negotiating, or trial work in a courtroom.

Most Goodies will tackle any assignment that doesn't require being assertive--such jobs are clerking, order-taking, secretary, assistant, line production employee--and any manual labor where job categories and responsibilities are well defined, such as painter, carpenter, or stagehand.

## Happiest when protected

Since they are followers, Goodies get along with almost anybody. They are happiest with an authority figure strong enough to stabilize their environment. Protected by a strong person, the Goody is given consistent direction as well as being shielded from competing authority figures--who can create problems of divided loyalty.

140

Example: A Goody secretary does an excellent job for one manager. When, in an economy move, she is given a second boss, she starts having difficulties as she tries to serve two masters. If other bosses are added to her responsibility, she becomes a nervous wreck. Because she is incapable of refusing the incessant demands of a number of bosses for priority for their work, she blows out her circuits in a vain and frantic attempt to please them all.

## Protection is essential

Goodies need protection from abuse, which is inflicted by others and themselves. To shield them:

• Make sure there aren't too many people making demands on the Goody. If pressed, the Goody will work until he becomes exhausted, which helps neither him nor the company.

• Hold down his work hours--even if he insists on working them. And don't allow him to cancel his vacations. Train your managers to spot this self-destructive behavior by the Goody.

• Don't permit managers to force a Goody into a promotion for a position he is unsuited to fill, especially if he is content and doing well in his current slot. The bigger job will quickly expose the failings of the player and render him a far less productive employee.

## Storing up anger

Goodies deeply involved in their game become so compulsive about complying that they try to bend over backward in multiple directions. This constant yearning to please creates a reserve of bitterness and resentment that they repress since they refuse to show any hostility.

On the job, these extreme players escape uncomfortable situations by becoming sick, often with the classic psychosomatic illnesses--headaches, stomach upsets. At the root of this behavior is the player's hostile-dependent relationship with his authority figure. He is angry at the very person he is most dependent on. One way to retaliate for this dependency is to develop phobias or debilitating depressions.

Hard-core players come from two types of parents--demanding and compliant. Some players had abrasive, demanding parents who absolutely refused to accept any deviance from the prescribed path, or even any questioning from the child. The Goody decided early that the only way to get along was to do everything the parents said.

Most hard-core players have mothers who were themselves Goodies. They train their children to be nice to everyone, no matter what. Since schools encourage and reward compliance, these players are praised for their placidity and friendliness. Such Goodies are model teenagers, which exasperates their more rebellious peers. The players get along, and make it--but they lose touch with their own creativity and intuition. Many never again regain it.

These players rarely seek solutions because they define their highly compliant behavior as normal. After all, it has served them well in life. Only after they fall victim to depression and psychosomatic illnesses do they realize that they have a problem. At such times they may be amenable to psychotherapy. They will also probably require assertiveness training to define themselves as individuals. Then they can realize their own needs and how to meet them while remaining cooperative with others.

142

Chapter Twenty

# FATHER KNOWS BEST

The head of a company regards his employees as his children--sons and daughters administered to and chided when necessary by their all-knowing Dad. Dynamic and highly aggressive, the Father is able to put together a successful enterprise. He hires many bright young children with great potential but no future, at least not with him. The types he attracts are limiting themselves by playing the game of DADDY WILL PROVIDE (page 149).

Although he occasionally longs for an equal, the Father's firm secret belief is that he has no peers. He is in charge not only of his own destiny but that of his company and employees. He's convinced that his workers would melt in the rain if it weren't for him.

If you run a large enough firm, you may have division heads playing Father. This player makes no bones about his willingness to take charge. He is affable, friendly, and helpful; he tries to help his employees with their work and also in their personal lives. He gives presents openly, sometimes within a short time of acquaintance. He is skilled at starting people talking about their problems, then announces that he has the solutions. He exudes an aura of authority and success and is likely to throw his arm around the shoulders of a colleague, while making such reassuring statements as, "That's okay, I'll take care of it."

As he gets deeper into the game, a Father tends to patronize his employees. He offers unnecessary, gratuitous advice and supervision and interferes even when his employees are perfectly capable of handling a problem without his help.

## Into everyone's business

Since Father can't delegate authority, he spends all his time plunging his hands into other people's business. This gives him too little time for himself. The harried Father thus lacks the quiet moments he needs to be creative, to think through problems, to consult with people, and to attempt the more complicated tasks that are part of his responsibility as a boss.

The constant worrying and fretting about the concerns of others increases stresses on the Father, which tends to interfere with his judgment, leading to poor and illogical decisions.

The Father stifles his employees, preventing them from ever developing to their full potential. This diminishes the level of performance in workers whose creativity is squashed.

Unwilling to be stifled, many of the most able employees leave the firm. The only skilled workers who remain are those who can manage to isolate or protect themselves in some way or other from the pervasive paternalism.

Father is often closed out by his own workers, who fear his interference and patronizing attitude. They hold back decisions and negative information in order to placate him. Trouble is, such withheld information may be vital. Being fed only the material that keeps him out of the way of his employees makes the Father less useful to the company.

## Comfort with Father

Fathers form a complementary relationship with adults who want a parent to watch over them. The grownups who play the kids' games find comfort under the wing of the all-providing Father. For paternalism to work, there must be compliant children-employees. Fortunately for Father, there are many out there willing to play the role.

When the game is played by a division manager, the solutions for this game are primarily structural; i.e., they lie in the way you place employees, order jobs, and manipulate the work environment. The boss can utilize a subordinate Father's strong desire to control by placing him in charge of routine functions--foreman of a section or chief of a group of clerks. This directs his passion for obtrusive involvement into the channels of thorough supervision. For workers performing jobs that aren't very exciting, Father's care and concern are more fully appreciated than by those engaged in more demanding and stimulating tasks.

If a Father happens to be in charge of creative workers, try to station him beyond easy reach of his employees. Put some real physical space be-

tween him and his workers so that they are free to think without his disrup-
tions. The Father shouldn't be allowed to view the work of his staff until
they have completed drafts, versions, or experiments. By contrast, if
Father is placed in the center of his creative work team, his obsessive desire to get his hands into every phase of the work will turn off his employees and nothing good will be forthcoming.

## The intentions are good

The intrusiveness of the Father, while the most negative aspect of
paternalism, is partly a sign of genuine interest, partly evidence of an
aching need for approval, involvement, and support. In no case does a
Father interfere malevolently; he doesn't mean to destroy or harm.

Thus his associates should be instructed to make clear contracts with
Father that limit the amount of contact and input he has with their work.
The contract provides a hard-and-fast aid in restricting the extent of
Father's intrusive behavior.

## An inward look

Fathers are aggressive, competent, and full of ideas. They need only
to be civilized. If you think you might be a Father, consider these approaches to the civilizing process:

• Increase your sensitivity to other people's desires, needs, ways
of functioning, and right to independence.

• Through self-awareness, recognize your need for approval but seek
it in a more direct, productive way rather than through playing a game of
obedience and compliance with your employees.

For you to lead everyone into adulthood requires an extremely dynamic relationship with a consultant who can serve as mentor. As the consultation proceeds and succeeds, your employees are released from the bondage of their games. Without you to depend on psychologically, your workers are forced to stand on their own. They are now allowed and encouraged to flourish into full-grown humans.

This program may be supplemented and supported by assertiveness training and teaching of other management skills so that the employees are fully competent to take on the new roles assigned to them.

As you learn to delegate authority, the employees feel better and better about caring for themselves and exercising their newly found competence.

Remember: Everybody's natural father has no peers. In order for the Father in this game to mature, he must allow his employee-kids to grow up. Let your workers accept responsibility, Dad. Don't waste your time chasing after the kids and changing their diapers.

## A shrewd precociousness

The Father who plays this game in its third degree was often an only or eldest child saddled prematurely with responsibility for which he wasn't prepared. His parents could have been childlike people who were saying, "I'll take care of you when I grow up," but never did. As a child, the player's shrewd precociousness made adults seem powerless.

Later, in early adulthood, the aggressive, hypercompetent future Father probably found that his ability to perform exceeded that of other workers. He then lost respect for the ability of others to assume responsibility and perform. He soon formed his lifelong attitude of, "I'm the only one who really knows how to do it right."

Ironically, Fathers harbor a secret desire to be taken care of by the real grownup they lacked attention from as children. This desire is constantly being tested against all competitors for the Father's position. But the Father always manages to thwart anyone who offers to take care of him--he becomes skilled at defeating the efforts of those who want to take charge of his life.

Then, convinced that only he has the secret truth, Father proceeds to construct his own world with people who are willing to believe in him. This confirms his isolation and his control over his dangerous, secret desire to be taken care of by someone.

In the most extreme form of this game, Father finally convinces himself that no one can do anything right but him. He then makes infants out of all those willing to put up with him within or outside the organization. Yet because he still secretly wants to be cared for, he tends to become an angry and querulous dictator. His game drives him to be more and more closed off from society, increasingly rigid, and less and less creative. In the terminal stages he reigns--isolated, crotchety, senile, refusing to retire since no one is good enough to take his place.

Chapter Twenty-One

# DADDY WILL PROVIDE

Like dependent children, some adults need a Daddy to care for them. Unwilling to face growing up, such people act the role of a Little Fella seeking a parent to protect him from the often harsh realities of the business world. The Little Fella tries to further his career--and maintain his job--through mutual psychological dependence (DADDY WILL PROVIDE) rather than hard work. The Little Fella is a master at playing on the needs of some bosses for a subordinate with a dependent, childlike personality. The Little Fella and the Daddy-Boss complement one another. One craves parental guidance and strength; the other wants a waif to care for.

## Its false assumptions

The game is predicated on two false assumptions:

1. There is an ideal parent who will watch out for the Little Fella.

2. The Little Fella can evade the consequences if the parent isn't ideal--or stops providing.

Example: An accountant seeking to please his Daddy-boss, the senior partner in the accounting firm, convinced him to start a computerized operation that he, the Little Fella, would run. The accountant claimed extensive computer expertise from an earlier job, although his experience was limited to a working knowledge of one type of machine. Since he was psychologically dependent on the approval of the Daddy-boss, the Little Fella stretched the truth to make Daddy proud.

The firm bought some $100,000 worth of computers and as much in software. When faced with this impressive display of material, the Little Fella failed miserably. He wasn't up to the promises he had made to the Daddy-boss, who ended up selling much of the new equipment.

The Little Fella then tried to make it up to the boss by taking potential clients out to lavish lunches to secure new business contracts. However, the entertainment gambit failed as a method of drumming up business, since quality of food, wine, and service is scarcely an accurate measure of an accounting firm's capabilities. And the concentration on the new approach didn't allow the Little Fella enough time to accomplish any accounting work in the office.

## Demands for forgiveness

The persistent attempts of the Little Fella to please demanded that the Daddy-boss be more and more forgiving. Eventually, the Daddy could forgive no more and the Little Fella was let go. This worked great hardship on the Daddy-boss, since it was like firing a favorite child. The Little

Fella was hurt too, but he had an excuse--he blamed the Daddy-boss for being uncaring.

## Skilled mind readers

Players have a knack: They can seemingly read the interviewer's mind and then state their abilities and interests in a form that exactly fits the interviewer's needs. In other words, whatever skills you need are precisely the ones the Little Fella has.

Although a Little Fella may be convincingly ingratiating with his "I'm just your man" approach, he tends to be fuzzy about details. He is vague about his past achievements and abstract when it comes to ways to implement fulfillment of the glowing goals he espouses. In his mind, this tactic leaves him open so that he can sense the niche that Daddy wants filled. In effect he is saying, "Tell me what you want and I'll be it." Unfortunately for both players, his talents don't always match his extravagant claims.

## An incongruous record

If their references are carefully checked, their glowing reports of past accomplishments may not be supported--although not vehemently contradicted either. There may be incongruities and discrepancies between the Little Fella's positive self-report and actual job performance. While the report was excellent, the record shows a mediocre-to-adequate performance level.

Extensive checking of the records will turn up an obvious pattern: the player may be productive--but he always promised far more than he could deliver. Often he will claim a desire for greater opportunity or challenge, especially when seeking a job in an entrepreneurial organization. Once again, past history betrays a need for dependent status: the record will show that the Little Fella has never gone out on his own to accept or perform challenging tasks.

## Ingratiating in failure

A player, faced with his failings, immediately becomes ingratiating. He pledges greater effort, finds imaginative excuses for his previous failures, and assures new dedication to his work.

Since he is incapable of delivering all that he promises, his self-justifications are empty talk. He lives in a fantasy world in which he imagines results that he can never achieve because he can't assemble a reasonable plan for performance.

A pleasant office personality, the Little Fella holds his position--to the extent that he can--through charm and friendliness. He knows the proper language and expressions that please and satisfy others. His enemies are few; he is skilled at positioning himself on the good side of everyone with whom he comes into contact; he is intuitive about the locations of power.

## Losing money on the little guy

The Little Fella drains money from the company--and bilks the boss--in several ways:

• The Daddy-boss pays the salary of a grownup with a child's foibles and irresponsibilities.

152

• In an effort to retrieve the Little Fella, the Daddy-boss may lay
out money for consultations and refresher courses and even cover up for
work undone.

• In extreme cases, the Little Fella can actually cost the Daddy-boss
his company. The Daddy-boss can invest great expectations in the Little
Fella. When these expectations fail to materialize, the Daddy-boss blames
himself. Some bosses have even decided to quit their businesses or seek new
directions for their lives.

## Brings out the negative

The Little Fella also bears responsibility for the psychological
cost of bringing out a negative side of the Daddy-boss. Since the Little
Fella never grows up or learns to care for himself, the Daddy-boss must
chastise him intermittently--which may lead to childish, angry outbursts
from the player. This cycle of demonstrated shortcoming, chastisement,
and temper doesn't promote a healthy working relationship.

## Use their affability

Any job that requires a maximum of affability and a minimum of productivity is suitable. Little Fellas can handle complaints well because they
are capable of soothing the complainer. This is useful when irritated
customers or clients must be stroked.

Keep Little Fellas away from any production-oriented position, especially if it is a critical function that can create a bottleneck--as in
manufacturing--or a crisis, such as in cash flow control, where a lack of
performance can lead to a catastrophe. Example:

A sales manager who's a Little Fella to his boss exaggerates his level of sales to justify the faith placed in him. The boss orders an increase of goods, and in response the plant's manufacturing gears up and produces increased inventory--for nonexistent sales. The grim result: too much product and no cash flowing in, all because the Little Fella wanted to please.

## Rely on contracts

To ensure that a Little Fella performs up to his ability, make a contract with him that states firmly specified goals. Then run checkups periodically to be certain that the contract is being honored through performance. If the Little Fella continues to fail to meet the terms of the contract and makes excuses and promises, fire him.

Place the Little Fella in jobs involving relationships with others. This may mean transferring him from production. But if he has the job skills for the department you put him in, you will improve his chance of remaining with the company.

A false solution for a larger corporation is to transfer the failing Little Fella into another, similar department. If the new department is also run by a Daddy-boss, the cycle may be repeated; if not, the departure-- and the general agony--has merely been postponed.

## Learning the game early

A Little Fella playing the extreme, or third-degree, form of this game learns early in life that to survive and prosper he need only stay on the good side of certain authority figures.

As a child, the Little Fella seems a spoiled brat to outsiders. In the family, however, he is seen as a lovable, if difficult, child throughout his school years. He continues to ingratiate himself with teachers in an effort to avoid the completion of assigned tasks. He relishes the role of teacher's pet.

Still, the work never quite gets done. Some players use illness in childhood as a ploy or excuse for lack of performance--an excuse they will transfer into their work career. Often they will have succeeded through cheating in school or plagiarizing the work of others. Careful selection of nondemanding "gut" courses enables them to avoid any difficult subject.

## Opting for easy jobs

Their early work history repeats the pattern of choosing easy tasks and creating unrealistic images of their achievements. They often even rob other people's ideas or steal their thunder by claiming respnsibility for accomplishments in which they had a minimal role, if any. Sooner or later, they are uncovered and resign, or are let go. As a result, they have a record of frequent job changes.

## Prescriptions for these players

Players generally won't undertake therapy to resolve the problem of being Little Fellas. They start treatment for other anxiety syndromes and the Little Fella role is picked up in the analysis. With help, the game can be kept under control by learning to live with it. The Little Fella shouldn't harass himself about not having great goals. He should enjoy life without guilt as long as he knows that when he grows up, he'll take on responsibility. (In this guise, and for younger people, this phase of the game may be called Sowing Wild Oats.)

Little Fellas must learn to stop making grandiose gestures. They must lower their expectations and do the things they like to do. For example, a Little Fella trying--and failing--to please a boss in a high-pressure company would do well to quit and start his own business, perhaps running a store or service. It's a relatively simple way to loosen the hold of the game.

## What about the game the Daddy-boss is playing?

It takes two to play the game of LITTLE FELLA. We have spoken primarily about what you as boss can do about the Little Fella. But what about the problem of the Daddy-boss?

Take the case of one who plays the game mildly: a strong, competent person who retains a lingering insecurity from childhood that is not ameliorated by his being good at his job. He is reluctant to confront workers who don't deliver productive work and readily accepts the excuses that those people (Little Fellas) make. By so doing, he becomes a player himself.

The conditioning for this type of behavior may occur when the player is raised in a household with at least one parent who is less competent than he is. Although this parent promised to take care of the child some day, the promise was never kept and the player was forced into becoming a grownup before his time.

(If you feel you are playing Daddy-boss, or see others in your office who are, chances are there is a dependent parent or two in the psychological background.)

156

## A split self-image

These extreme players are the victims of a split between a glamorous self-image and a deep, fearful insecurity. To support an overinflated ego and protect their highly vulnerable inner selves, they require a retinue of flatterers and hangers-on. This creates a secure image: holding court, being loved, having appreciative listeners--and possessing supreme authority.

To the businessman who finds himself in this position, the costs are tremendous and can be ruinous to his company.

## Solutions for the Daddy-boss:

These players are not interested in help as long as they are able to maintain their false worlds, where they are the center of attention. They don't define the situation as a problem; they see it as their just due. Players seek help only in severe depression--after their universe has collapsed, i.e., when their ability to produce wealth through their enterprise cannot keep up with the costs of their retinue.

Under these circumstances, the treatment is identical to that available for depression, including psychotherapy, with careful review of the personality disorder that led to the problem. Primarily, the solution is a working through of the insecurity so that competent Daddy-bosses can ease out of the game and become able to enjoy their competence instead of squandering it.

## Putting the game to work

Many facets of this game can be used toward business success. Daddy-bosses are very productive people, for example. They are esteemed during the early phases of their careers. Before they collapse into extreme behavior, they need to be carefully controlled as to the size of the retinue they construct around them.

For a manager: review and listen to advice of accountants and consultants. Pare down all unnecessary and excessive personnel. If this proves difficult or impossible, psychotherapy to examine basic insecurity and anxiety is an answer.

Part Four

# PESSIMISTIC SECURITY GAMES

Those who play these games feel that life is a losing proposition. The best they can do is to slow down the tempo and hang on. There is scant hope-- or desire--to push oneself toward higher goals. Surviving is the name of the game and keeping whatever security the player has is the driving force. So widespread is this attitude, however, that the section includes some of the most common games played by employees.

# Chapter 22

# SACRED
# COW

A Sacred Cow can drain the life blood of a business. He occupies an important position, often high in the hierarchy, where he impedes vital decisions and stifles innovation. In spite of the debility he creates, however, he is held in high esteem by the corporate power structure. He is venerated much as is the sacred cow in India, where cattle are holy. They do anything they want, immune from virtually all prohibitions. Yet while a sacred cow in India can be useful as a draft animal and giver of milk, the Sacred Cow in business is a dead loss.

To get where he is, the Sacred Cow makes himself crucial to a company as he passes through three stages: ingratiation, institutionalization, and sanctification. In the process, he comes to believe that past performance is a license to stop being productive.

First, the Sacred Cow ingratiates himself with the company management through bursts of work, shrewd friendships, family connections, or respect earned from success in a previous job.

Next, he is institutionalized through promotion to a position of command--vice president or partner. Finally, sanctification comes through longevity in the company. The Sacred Cow is adept at survival. He assumes the aura of one blessed and armored against most pressures to change--or to leave.

## Status with time

Many Sacred Cows achieve identifiable status late in their careers; potential types are not easy to pick out before hiring. One variety is discoverable, however: the VIP from another company who is already a star before the initial job interview. He may have had important family or business connections in the earlier job, have been a leader for a competitor, or served as the head of a company now merged with yours.

## Some ways executives become Sacred Cows

A consultant who helps your organization out of a severe problem is hired, as a reward, for a managerial post in your company. For example, your accounting is done by an outside firm. As your company grows, the accounting firm takes on more and more of your work load. Finally, you decide that because the head of the accounting firm is so skilled at balancing your books, you'll hire him to head an Accounting Division. In time, the head accountant becomes a Sacred Cow who ends up impeding your business growth.

What happened? The period of ingratiation occurred when the accountant did good work for your company. Institutionalization came about through growth, which created a need for full-time accounting help; the accountant himself was institutionalized by being hired. The accountant was then sanctified by his long and positive history of helping your company--and by just remaining in his job month after month, year after year. You may hear yourself saying, "Arnold gave up his own business to come and be my chief accountant. I owe him plenty." To prove it, you have given Arnold a cushy, long-term berth.

Arnold has it made. Before he even steps into your office as a full-time employee he enjoys a good reputation and your obvious gratitude. If you don't watch out, Arnold may bask in his past accomplishments and the Accounting Division could become your weakest.

Other examples:

A manufacturing company that has been using independent representatives decides to hire the best of the reps to head its regional sales department. These entrepreneurs, with solid reputations as salesmen, don't fit into the company structure. Soon sales are off but the regional sales heads who aren't fired may have become Sacred Cows.

Any time a company buys out a supplier and gives the chief operating officer of the company a position, it runs the risk of creating a Sacred Cow.

After a job interview, check the records of the applicant carefully. He might have been a Sacred Cow at his last job and is now searching for a new barn. The job record will reveal the cycle: good job with a subsidiary company, say, with promotion to an executive position; then a general falloff in performance, to the detriment of the main company.

Beware: a Sacred Cow who has achieved stardom with another company knows how to sell himself. Don't let him talk you into hiring him precipitously. Make no promises until you go over his records carefully.

## A cow stands out

In any office, a Sacred Cow is highly visible. He may be an aging founder or president. He's the one who gets away with costly, destructive practices, even though he is ostensibly conforming to normal business procedures. He shows up late, leaves early, and spends much of his time in nonproductive activities--reading newspapers, drinking coffee, and preventing otherwise productive employees from doing their work. He is never reprimanded, however, because he is untouchable.

When his failings are brought to the attention of superiors, they murmur and bow down before the Sacred Cow. And criticism is deflected by a detailed account of why the Sacred Cow is untouchable.

## How he drains money

The Sacred Cow may seem harmless, an executive whose only expense to the company is his padded salary. But he can run up many other costs:

• Primarily, the inefficiency of having a nonperforming employee in an important slot.

• The negative reaction to be expected from employees who see a deadhead raised beyond criticism. This has direct organizational costs--in lowered productivity and lowered morale.

• Occasionally, the Sacred Cow will launch obscure and absurd projects--to exercise his authority or to fend off boredom. These projects can consume a disproportionate amount of resources.

Example: A Sacred Cow manager is convinced that playing softball will heighten company morale. Soon he has the whole factory out on the ball field, even during productive hours. Next come the fancy uniforms, high-priced equipment, and picnics after the games. In no time, the factory is a ball club and corporate managers are wondering, "Do they make anything or just play ball?" Thus a morale builder, dreamed up by a strong-willed Sacred Cow, becomes a money waster.

## Distinguished, personable

Sacred Cows are often charming. Distinguished, dignified, and personable, they mix well with almost all types. Indeed, it is their skill at personal relations that helped them attain their high status and maintain their position. People are not their problem.

## Hard-headed detractors

Some associates won't buy the line put out by the Sacred Cow. They include tough-minded production people who, as clear thinkers, are resistant to his game.

## Some tough solutions

Since the Sacred Cow is often so personable, the solutions can be tough on a boss. Show the player you are aware of what he is and help him seek an honorable way of withdrawing from the company. The following are examples of Sacred Cows who were removed by managers:

• A man who had founded his own business was sadly past his prime. His stubbornness and intractability hobbled the company's growth. His son, the most productive executive employee, went to the company's bank and told its directors he would resign unless his father, the Sacred Cow, was put out to pasture. The bank directors knew the company couldn't maintain productivity--and keep up its loan payments--without the son. The bank directors requested the father's retirement and threatened to withhold their line of credit if he refused. The Sacred Cow gave in and accepted the honorific title of Chairman of the Board; the son took over leadership as president and chief operating officer.

• A corporation bought out its main supplier, thinking that corporate ownership would make the operation more efficient. Once it was brought in-house, however, the supply operation lost efficiency as the manager became a Sacred Cow. Since the parent company depended on the supplier, there seemed no ready answer.

Then, the parent company devised a shrewd move: it sold the supply company to the men who managed it. The supply firm regained its vitality as it moved back into its former role as a dynamic entrepreneurial business. In an exceptional reform, the manager shed his role and image of Sacred Cow, and the supply company became its old efficient self.

## Are you a Sacred Cow?

Most Sacred Cows don't recognize the game they are playing. You might ask yourself these questions:

• Do you ever say to yourself, "I've got it made"?

• Do you feel that you could get away with just about anything you wanted? (Have you already?)

If the answer to these questions is yes, you could be a Sacred Cow.

## Players are spoiled brats

A Sacred Cow whose continued presence can lead to the demise of the corporation is a hard-core player. Basically, such a player is a spoiled brat.

When young, the player was often a favorite child, someone encouraged to believe he was special. His wants were considered above those of others. The good things he did were praised as exceptional while the bad were quickly excused.

Instead of growing and learning, the hard-core player continues the role of brat, which results in an increasing need to hide the truth from himself in order to maintain self-esteem.

Example: An entrepreneur's son can easily become a hard-core player. Not by learning his job, but through influence, he advances through the company his father built. His name enables him to wield power, yet he doesn't really contribute anything to the business. He can't be criticized by those who know more than he does, yet he can make disastrous business decisions. His father went from rags to riches; the son will return the riches to rags if he becomes a diehard Sacred Cow.

## Hard-to-reach players

Because of their narcissistic personalities, these players are hard to reach through psychotherapy. They refuse to recognize the character of the game they play, because their problems have seldom been brought to their attention. When they do seek therapeutic exploration, it is usually because of the pain of disruptive personal relationships created by their me-first attitude.

Even when approaching a therapist, they may claim to be above it:
"Doctor, some people have been telling me that there's something wrong
with me," one might say. "I don't believe them. You listen and tell me if you
think there's anything wrong." If they can find a therapist who is smarter,
tougher, and quicker than they are, these spoiled brats can grow up and become responsible exercisers of their true abilities.

Chapter 23

# "HELL, I'M ONLY HUMAN"

In the eyes of players of this game, just being human excuses mistakes of every sort. Every time they do something wrong, rather than admit to error, they reassure themselves by saying, "Hell, I'm only human." In this way, they compensate themselves for the consequences of self-imposed limitations.

While this line of reasoning may satisfy the player, it is difficult for a manager to counter without appearing inhuman himself. Thus, mistakes are not recognized; the player may never learn from his errors. At every attempt to upgrade his ability to perform, the player resists the manager. His rationale for his actions is that any attempt at improving his skills flies in the face of his humanness. This passive attitude does not lead to an eager, energetic working relationship between the game player and his boss.

## How does a player get hired?

Those who play this game are usually signed on during a personnel crunch. Sometimes they come aboard through managerial carelessness, friendship, or nepotism. The more glib player can sometimes convince you that any trouble in his previous job was the fault of others. He'll claim that all he needs is a fresh working environment.

Many players are hired because they apply for jobs that are beneath their talents.

Important: Not all players carry their game with them; some companies create players from vulnerable employees. If a corporation is destructive of its employees' self-esteem, it can grind down workers until they start playing this defensive game. In these circumstances, the harried employee's cry need not be a negative defense, but may be a counterattack and a plea for understanding. The wise boss will listen and take heed.

## A failure to follow through

The true player seldom plans for success. He tends to react to circumstance rather than anticipating triumphs, allowing predictable costs to pile up.

Here's an example: a player makes a suggestion for a way to make the mail operation more efficient during times of seasonal rush, such as at Christmas. Sure that his bosses will ignore him, he doesn't bother to work out the details of the scheme. When his suggestion is greeted favorably, the player starts to back off, make excuses, and stall. Time is lost and enthusiasm dies.

The player also usually has a shaky work record, since he tends to indulge himself through reporting sick, sometimes when most needed at work. His excuse rationale enables him to interpret minor physical ailments as incapacitating.

When confronted with his failings, the player likes to scapegoat. That means he gets his fellow workers in trouble needlessly, which causes animosity that can interrupt the work process and lead to costly delays.

Placed in a supervisory capacity, the player is a bust because he encourages his workers to play his game, excusing everyone's mistakes and ensuring poor performance down the line.

## Where can you place these players?

Ideal slots for employees with this problem are routine jobs that are slightly below their level of actual competence. Try to provide as much direct supervision as possible.

Example: An engineer schooled and trained as a machine designer allows his game to cripple him. Rather than let him go, try him as head of a maintenance crew where his ability with machines can be utilized for overseeing repairs. This may be a step down for the player, but with the pressure for innovation off him, he may flourish--assuming you supervise him carefully and help him with administration.

Similarly, some salesmen flop in carving out new districts or in pushing new products. But they can serve admirably as simple order-takers for existing lines in proven territories.

Resist any temptation to place these players in positions that require creativity, stamina, and rapid response in a crisis. When over-matched in this way, players put their energy into inventing excuses for failing rather than devising ways to complete the job.

## Heightening the sense of worth

Strong leadership and positive reinforcement can help a player shake free from the mild form of this game. You can also give him a heightened sense of his own worth through carefully structured contracts and career planning that establishes attainable goals. Once the player proves to himself that he can be an achiever, he starts to feel better about his abilities. Soon he may be willing to take on more work with expanded responsibilities.

Obviously, it should be company policy to discourage the acceptance of constant excuses. Under such a policy, individual players can either grumble along, like Archie Bunker, or seek psychotherapy. Once the player learns that rewards follow when he takes risks and succeeds, he will drop the game of convincing himself that his inadequacy is due to his membership in the human race. Unless he changes his attitude toward himself in this positive way, he is liable to fall for the quick fix offered by the game of TRUE BELIEVER (page 130).

## How associates can help the player

But insight into his problem may not completely solve the problem. A clear work contract that the player fulfills may be needed to complete the cure. Colleagues should be supportive when a player draws up such a contract and then meets its obligations. If the player reaches into his old grab bag of excuses, associates must remind him that this talk only masks the real issues.

In helping the player, fellow workers can help themselves. It's healthy for all your workers to be goal-oriented, and for you to let them know how these aims will be achieved. If they are willing to face a player on this subject, they will be more aware of their own sense of direction.

## Demanding, inconsistent parents

The player who is deeply involved in his game probably had critical parents who demanded more than he could deliver. Often, these parents asked for precocious behavior, then compounded the problem by failing to back the child up for his actual accomplishments. Though the parents regarded him as not up to snuff, the child's excuses were accepted. As the child developed skill in justifying inadequacy, he also developed low self-esteem and no clear definition of--or desire for--achievement. He emerged as an adult who hoped that his excuses would secure him the rewards that his meager efforts could not.

Chapter 24

# ONLY I KNOW
# WHERE IT IS

The production manager of a company that wholesaled manufacured oil-derivative products--lubricating oil, gasoline--designed and oversaw construction of a processing-warehouse complex. In this facility, refined oil was formulated into various retail products and pumped into drums, labeled, and stored. The complex was a marvel of modern technological design.

The problem was, only the production manager understood how it all worked. There was no master plan that could be understood by anyone except him. His office, instead of being a clean, efficient center of operations, was a shambles: his desk, furniture, floors, and walls were littered with sample cans, drums, technical journals, trade papers, and old invoices. Even the manager had trouble finding his way around the place.

The refinery only worked properly when the manager was there to over-

see it. He was always too busy to explain his system to a responsible subor-
dinate--but never so busy he couldn't complain about those who interfered
in his operation.

## Manager runs the show

Everybody in the organization depended on the manager. Luckily for
the business, he was a workaholic who was always on the job. But if he ever
took a day off or left the plant, nothing could function.

The owner, founder, and chief operating officer of the company also
fell under the control of the manager, who insisted that nothing could be
done in the plant without his OK. Thus, it was questionable whether the
owner actually owned anything at all. In any case, he had little control
over his own plant.

The manager had everything--plant, product, management, and em-
ployees--in his grip. They were all caught up in the game called ONLY I KNOW
WHERE IT IS.

In this game, an individual makes himself irreplaceable. Usually active in production (like the plant manager), finance, or personnel, the
player creates a system of manufacturing, storage, filing, contacts, or
communication that only he comprehends--and thus controls. The player is
competent and hard-working, but he trusts no one else to accomplish what he
can.

## How a player tips his hand

The status of this applicant as a player is easy to miss because he
presents himself as he basically is--a conscientious, technically

174

skilled workaholic who's eager to please. Only if he's old enough to have run through the game at least once in a previous job can he be diagnosed through careful evaluation of records and contact with former employers.

The player may tip his hand during the interview by his expressed interest in his measure of control of the job situation. He might ask as direct a question as: "How much power will I have in running my area?" More likely, the question will be: "Whom do I have to report to, and how often?" The applicant may also say, "I like to do things the way I think is right. I assume I'll be given a free hand to get things done my way." Caveat: this kind of remark may not, by itself, reveal the player; normally ambitious people also want responsibility and authority. However, a true player will not let the subject alone. The crucial stage of any interview comes when you ask the applicant if there is anything else about the company he'd like to know before you end the conversation. It is now that the applicant is likely to let slip some hints about the game he plays. In this case, the player will return to the topic of control. To whom will he be answerable? Will they tie his hands or allow him to run his own show?

It is hard to catch a player at the interview stage, however, because the game is customarily an acquired one--players grow into it on the job.

## A player in action

The player flags himself in several obvious ways:

• His office is full of stuff--papers, samples, piles of materials needed for his department. Only he can find a way through the mess--and sometimes even he is defeated by it.

• Anyone with a briefcase more than a foot wide is a player. His briefcase is always jammed with homework since only he knows how things run, and only he can do the work necessary to run them.

• His day is consumed by people asking his instructions about matters they long ago should have been left to decide for themselves. Anything out of the ordinary must be handled as a crisis since only the player knows where the fire extinguishers--and everything else--are hidden.

## Always late

• The player may often remind the onlooker of the frantic March Hare in Alice in Wonderland, who rushes about madly consulting his pocket watch and crying out, "I'm late!"

Reevaluate your managers with this job profile in mind: at first, the player enhances the growth of the company through his labors. He is awarded with additional help, which he manages badly. As his department struggles, more help is hired, yet productivity fails to increase. To justify him-self, the player spends much of his time keeping his employees in the dark about the operation. He even initiates internal squabbles among his workers to deflect attention from the department's workings--and fail-ings. In this chaos, he maintains sole, total control.

## Expensive game

This game can drain your company. It may even become so frustrating to deal with that you give up and sell out. Short of that, however, here are some of the day-to-day expenses:

• Since only the player understands the entire operation, his time is your money.

176

• He has real and ready excuses for frequent failures, all of which seem valid because so many operations go through his hands and he lacks the time to accomplish each properly.

• The costly system perpetuates itself since the one man who understands it has no time to teach anyone else how it works.

• Other managers are short-circuited by an inability to operate within the system.

• Incalculable costs accrue when the player is away on vacation or becomes ill--perhaps breaking down under periodic crisis--and his department ceases functioning. At that point, his area resembles a disturbed anthill more than a modern business operation.

## Suited for machines

These skilled production employees excel in any job that requires the hard reality of machines and production rather than people. In fact, they are so good at innovative use of machinery and applying math and theory in setting up operations that they tend to be promoted to the management of other employees who are less proficient. This is the basic mistake, however, since the players are geniuses with machinery and duds as managers.

Example: A line inspector at an oil refinery can watch dials all day to anticipate trouble and make repairs in case of malfunction. He is so good at his job that he is promoted to foreman. He now manages the other line inspectors--and his troubles begin.

Another example: A factory superintendent knows the physical plant from basement to roof, up one side and down the other. There isn't a lock or light he can't repair quickly and efficiently. He soon becomes foreman of maintenance, and falls into the game. He squirrels away his tools for fear his men might lose them. He keeps all the keys to the plant doors in his office--and locks the door. Only he holds the master key. He jealously guards his preserve by conceiving complex operations that only he understands. No work can proceed without him--even his most trusted employees are kept in the dark because he doesn't trust them to do the work right.

## Not a supervisor of people

No job that involves the supervision of other people or communication with other departments should be given this player. Keep him where he's best--working with things.

Basically, they don't really mesh with people at all: they mesh with objects, such as machines and tools. They only tolerate sycophants who will take their orders and in periods of crisis be grateful that the player is "in charge"--and not they.

## No man is indispensable

The foremost solution for this game is prevention. Nip in the bud any urge to put the player in a position where he becomes unassailable as the head of a department that he runs his own way without answering directly to anyone.

Remember: Any system, new or old, must be able to function for a while in the absence of its manager. If you sense that one manager is becoming truly indispensable, act quickly to end the game. Though he may have accrued a lot of power, don't fear him. Demand specific reforms.

• You're entitled to know how your business operates. The system must

be explained fully through charts, plans, and written instructions that
anyone--especially you--can understand. If the player pleads that he is
too busy for such work, give him an ultimatum: deliver or leave.

• Demand that all messes, including the one in the player's office,
be cleaned up within a definite period of time.

• The department must be reorganized with authority delegated to key
managers or subordinates. Employees must be trained and supervised to
function efficiently and knowledgeably within the department.

Example: Jimmy, the maintenance foreman who won't show anyone how the
office plant operates, must be brought into line. Make him construct a
board on which all keys hang with clear labels. Similarly, tools must be
conspicuously labeled. Boxes full of materials must display lists of their
contents on their tops, and diagrams of all the factory machines and maps of
the plant must be readily accessible. If these materials must be kept under
lock and key for security reasons, then you, as the boss, must have your own
key.


## Reform or out

These reforms may be impossible for the player to institute. After
all, he's a completely dedicated, loyal employee who has done a good job
while magnifying his own worth. But the player must reform even if it means
placing his job on the line.

In some cases, a consultant may be able to smooth the transition for
the player from petty chieftain back to responsible employee. The point is
to open up the department so that its workings are obvious to all those with
responsibility for it.

Be careful. This game may begin as a small annoyance, but sometimes bosses who have allowed managers to take over vital operations have had to go out of business in order to solve the problem. Only in this way have they been able to start from scratch with a system over which they exercise full authority.

## Prickly personality

Players often have abrasive personalities as well as being close-mouthed and noncommunicative. Their associates, therefore, need support and encouragement from you.

The clogged lines of communication between the player and his colleagues can be cleared through specific work contracts and follow-up. When everyone in the department knows what he is expected to do, nobody need hang on the whim of a player.

Teach the player to delegate authority, and require him to provide training for his fellow workers. These measures will let in light and air and help everyone perform better.

## If the manager plays

If the player is the founder or top manager of an unwieldy corporation, he should get out while he can and get involved with a smaller operation that he can run out of his hat. If he decides to stay, he must undertake consultation with outside experts and study of modern management techniques to learn how to reorganize the company, instituting, among other things, the delegation of some of his responsibilities to others. He must also set up a clear business structure with logical lines of communication and written policies, and with responsible employees in key positions.

## Background of a serious player

Someone who plays this game in the third degree is similar to a paranoid (page 93) but is more competent on the job and less rabid. He grew up in a family where self-reliance was essential for survival; if he didn't fend for himself, no one else would. Often this child fixed his own meals from an early age and took care of his clothing, books, transportation, and many basics starting with preschool. He was not abused by his parents, as in the case of a paranoid, but was neglected.

Such players survive by their precocious ability to gather vital information, which evolves as something precious that is not to be freely given to others. Hard-core players reproduce at work the atmosphere in which they were raised. As kids they were forced to look out for themselves; as players, they regard fellow workers as both unworthy of receiving and incapable of carrying out delegated assignments.

## Realizing the trouble

He usually won't recognize that he has a problem--the game has been ingrained since childhood. But until he shows signs that he is willing to recognize it as a problem and do something about it through consultation or therapy, he must be restricted to nonsupervisory, technical positions. Even then, he must be held accountable for where everything is. This will mean some overseeing on the part of his manager or you, but if he's technically competent, he may well a valuable enough employee to be worth the effort.

## Abide by the Peter Principle

Fortunately, the solutions to this game demand no change of personality. If a player wants to do managerial work, he must commit himself to learning organizational skills and the ability to communicate with people.

The player needs to abide by the lessons of the Peter Principle--and not take the promotion that carries him beyond his competence. If he's happy in technical fields, he should stay there. Not everyone has to become a manager.

## Learning the three stages

The game basically breaks down to three stages, each of which can be overcome with consultation.

The most extreme stage is the player who is an outright bottleneck--who won't allow things to flow through and out of his department.

A player in a milder stage puts his hands on too many operations. He can be disruptive to efficient workers and impede the running of things, but he isn't a bottleneck.

The preferred stage is the conscientious worker who wants to be in all phases of the job but doesn't get in the way. Players at this level of the game are usually prized employees.

# BUT AT LEAST, HANGING ON, GOOD OLD SAM

Although each of the following games is distinct, they are related. One leads into the other, even though it may take the player 20 years to evolve from BUT AT LEAST through HANGING ON to arrive at GOOD OLD SAM. Nor should this trio of games be dismissed as an aberration. Most people in the country's work force are playing one of them; they are the most prevalent games found in today's business world.

The series starts with BUT AT LEAST, a mild game in which the player decides to settle at a level comfortably below expectations. The game's slogan is one of mollification: "We may not be going places in our work, but at least we still have jobs."

Once a player chooses this safe stance, he is vulnerable to HANGING ON (page 190). In this game the player switches from safety to static self-defense. He clings to the job that provides him with security, not stimulation. Finally, the Hanger-On is transformed into GOOD OLD SAM (page 196), a human institution who is as much a part of the business as the furniture or machinery, and about as upwardly mobile.

Since these games are so common, it behooves any manager to understand their anatomy and cures. The point is to deflect the worker from settling by keeping alive his sense of quest and desire for challenge.

The player joins your company as a bright, enthusiastic worker who sprouts optimism. Yet after a period of testing, he opts for the safety of the sure job rather than the risks of advancing through bold or imaginative actions. His optimism remains intact, however. Even though he has settled for tasks that never test his true capacities, he can excuse away his lack of striving--and even his failures--with a smile: "We lost the big contract, but at least they're not suing us."

This false optimism is contagious, spreading reassurance for those who simply want to get by. Yet, with his enthusiasm, the player often convinces his boss that they share the same goals--and the same drive to achieve them. But through the actual mechanism of the game, the player protects himself from having to make much of an effort. Typical situations:

The boss posts a list of minimum standards that every employee must live up to. While outwardly agreeing with the boss's intent, the player inwardly interprets this list as a schedule of maximum performance necessary to retain his job.

A worker with a number of areas of responsibility cares for only those that demand the most pressing immediate attention. He'll allow the others to slide until they reach a state of crisis that requires emergency treatment. When confronted about permitting matters to slip from his control, he'll reply, "But at least I took care of the crisis areas."

For example, a sales manager feels his bosses want increased sales. He sends out his men with new quotas and devotes all his efforts toward pushing them to the top. Meanwhile, his paperwork falls behind. Only when it reaches crisis proportions does he attend to it--and then he drops the sales effort. His flawed goal: to please his superiors without coordinating his sales push and paperwork so that he'll really be in charge.

Note: In its milder versions, BUT AT LEAST is not a lifelong game. It frequently occurs among workers who don't want to be doing what they are being paid to do. Perhaps that's why it's such a common game in today's business community.

Learn to spot it early, particularly among employees who you feel have a future in your firm. If the game is nipped in the bud, the player can easily be saved as a productive, growing worker.

## Reliable workers

Players are stable, quiet, industrious, and make no waves. Invariably, they will choose the routine job over the more risky, higher-paying one. They are the managers so satisfied with organizational housework that they seldom attempt anything creative.

## The price of "settling"

In the short term, this game is cost-free. The player makes his fellow workers feel good, particularly about their ability to survive. Whenever workers might feel doubts about a poorly realized job, the player will console them with, "We did pretty good, considering..."

Eventually, this attitude costs your business money. One is the missed opportunity papered over by the player: "We could have made $5 million on that deal, but at least we cleared $50,000."

The player is reactive--he responds only to stimuli. He isn't proactive--that is, he doesn't anticipate or become aggressively involved with new concepts. This means that when the opportunity arises to close a better deal or raise the stakes for more profit, the player hangs back. He is content with the safety of the known. This kind of underachieving is reflected in the profit and loss columns when you realize what might have been if only the player had tried harder or been more alert to the company's best interests. The ultimate cost to your company is that it never has the benefit of the player's full output.

## Encouraging the player to get out of his rut

Warning: Do not be tempted to promote the player past his level of effectiveness. It's an easy trap to fall into because he is a faithful, loyal employee who induces intense feelings of obligation. Instead of moving him up, reward him with a better salary. If you feel he could handle increased responsibility, suggest that the player attend courses to strengthen his personality. The player who wants to break out of this game can benefit from the Human Potential movement.

Sometimes, switching jobs can help the player find the courage to take more risks. Indeed, the very act of changing jobs is a sign of initiative. The player must realize that he needn't accept a "survival performance" as his maximum professional effort.

Encourage all division and group heads to press players to take calculated risks. Hold periodic meetings in which workers are urged to display initiative in everything from new production techniques to ways of performing the most routine jobs in a more efficient manner.

Get the player involved in day-to-day operations to make him realize that the business is more than just his specialized task. Explain the current crisis and what caused it. If increased productivity on his part can help the company, request his cooperation. Introduce him to the excitement of breaking out of his trap of minimum-level execution.

## Reentry problems

People who are returning to the work force after a prolonged absence are unsure of their capacities and will often take up this game for defense. This is true of women who have finished raising families and have returned to work. In their cases, the game can be tolerated for a period. Thereafter, players must be obliged to take risks so that the game doesn't become a permanent part of their work attitude.

## A special message to a boss

Some managers play this game without quite realizing it. It's not hard to see how it might work: say you're 63, too young to retire, and yet bored--too familiar with your company's workings to give it your all. After a deep soul-search, you could come up with these choices: (a) sell the business and retire; (b) bring in new blood at the management level; (c) kick yourself upstairs and sign on a new chief operating officer. Another solution is to sell the part of the business that bores you and concentrate on areas that start your juices flowing.

Remember: Just because you run things doesn't mean that you can't fall into the habit of settling for less than top performance.

## Reviving quashed expectations

Players who cling to this game usually came from families that specialized in low expectations. The positive side of any catastrophe was emphasized and the child's mistakes and failures were seldom criticized.

The main negative force in the family was the indirect quashing of the child's expectations. The parents feared overachievement, so they encouraged the child to aim for the level beneath his skills. They constantly told the child, "That's too hard for you," or, "Why don't you try something simpler?"

The child learned that to please his parents, he need never extend himself or take any chances. In fact, the more conservatively he behaved, the more he was rewarded.

Warning: These players are highly susceptible to becoming True Believers (page 130). Their attraction for routine tasks dovetails with a charismatic leader's gift for holding sway over those of low expectations.

## Good slots for players

These players can perform ordinary jobs without complaining. As long as they aren't pushed beyond their capacities, they can form the backbone of your work staff. Advance them only after they have been given special personality training.

Some older, established companies make an unspoken policy of hiring and promoting But At Leasters. A company that enjoys a self-renewing market share with a product that's a household word does not generally attract dynamic leaders, once the founding entrepreneurs pass on. Management and workers tend to be interested in safety and security as they say, "We won't quarrel with proven success."

In the best-run of such mature companies, that may be fine. Indeed, because a product is well established, radical approaches might well scare off the customers.

Chapter 26

# HANGING ON

Anyone who has been unable to stop playing BUT AT LEAST can easily move along to HANGING ON. This is a position of defense that consists of holding onto a job that may have been rewarding in the past but now provides only safety and comfort.

The Hanger-On is intuitively aware that the time has come for him to move on--find work that challenges and excites him. While convincing himself that he will, he scares himself into staying. He constantly awaits the arrival of some magical event that will free him.

Occasionally, the player is blasted loose by Reality. He realizes that if he doesn't start taking risks, he will never grow. And once he has made the change, chances are he will be delighted both with his work and himself--even though he probably resisted the shift bitterly.

The nature of HANGING ON is rooted in the dread and pessimism that the player feels about his chances for success. His fear grows from this pattern at work: The player starts his career at a company with a period of successes--there is a good fit between him and his responsibility. At length, he knows that he is at a job he has mastered. Instead of moving higher, however, he is held in place by a lack of opportunities or a series of lateral assignments. Here's an example of a player locked into HANGING ON:

A manufacturer's representative works for a company whose product--cutlery--is very stable. About all the representative can do is compete on price, which he does and earns a decent living. However, the markets he created for the product are solid, the company is profitable, and there seems to be no way to make his work more exciting. He is stuck in a respectable job that he can do with his eyes closed.

What are his alternatives to HANGING ON?

1. He can join a new company with a product that is more varied, with more potential for opportunity. The player, however, fears failure and he does not want to abandon a good position for such a great risk.

2. He could start his own company to sell complementary--or competing--products to his loyal buyers. This is even more frightening to the player.

3. He could augment his line of cutlery by serving as a representative for other companies making related--but not competing--goods. This would mean increasing his work load by attending more trade shows and actively seeking quality goods to sell. Seriously contemplating the choice, the representative was at first reluctant. But eventually he decided that such a course was his best chance to rid himself of HANGING ON. He found several new lines of products that he represented along with his cutlery. He

opened new markets, is busier than ever, proud of himself, and making good money--more than he was before.

## Staleness starts the game

The tragedy of the Hanger-On is that he enters the company highly motivated and wanting to succeed. His game starts after his initial triumphs. As staleness sets in, his priorities shift from learning, growth, and performance to overt courting of security. The longer the player stays in the HANGING ON position, the easier it is to stay longer.

He is like a character in Eugene O'Neill's play The Iceman Cometh, in which the habitues of Harry Hope's rundown bar talk about what they will accomplish "some day." Faced with reality, however, they retreat into the comfort of their dreams. Similarly, the Hanger-On glows with enthusiasm about what he will do "some day." He even believes his own lies. Often, Hangers-On congregate--as in the play--to reassure one another with their dreams of a better day.

## Luck vs. success

The player's speech leans toward the subjunctive: "If only..." and "If I were free of this job..." It is padded with excuses, justifications, and vague longings: "With one lucky break I'll be out of this dump."

Any story of someone who has "made it" is eagerly embraced. Yet, without help of some sort, the player's plans for getting out or "making it" are seldom implemented.

Hangers-On are found in every profession, even the most glamorous--movie studios, television networks, theater, advertising, publishing,

journalism, Wall Street. More often, the game serves as an outlet to help
workers survive the dreary days of dead-end jobs, such as factory and as-
sembly-line work.

## The heavy burdens of carrying dead wood

While the player is placid and tractable, he can be cost-free to the
company as he completes his hack work without a whimper. The company suffers the long-term burden, however, of carrying dead wood--rather than enjoying the benefit of a lively, innovative employee.

As the game takes hold of the player, he suffers increased depression, decreased motivation, and a narrowing of his concentration until it
focuses solely on his job. This makes him a weak link in times of stress. It
also means that his problems tend to become chronic--typically resulting
in loss of work time and a lack of mental and emotional presence when on the
job.

The extra cautious attitude of the player can stifle those around him
and hold them back. As he talks of what he'll do "some day," his dreams seem
more and more unreal. The cumulative effect is to dilute the hopes of others
who may not be so deeply committed to the game, keep them from making contributions to the success of the company, and even throttle their own
dreams for advancement or personal achievement.

## Moving off dead center

To prevent such a situation from developing, have an active career
counseling service available to employees. Or hire an on-call consultant
who can work around the issues of career-planning with eligible employees

and management. The point is to help the Hanger-On move off dead center by focusing his attention on his ability to handle risks.

Often real solutions, arrived at with counseling, are quite creative. Most players have talents that they pursue as avocations, or hobbies, that can be incorporated into their careers.

Example: A salesman who reached a dead end at his job was discovered to possess a high level of mechanical skills. He started selling a line of machinery that he was able to master for his customers while explaining its technical advances. His personal skills gave him an edge that other salesmen lacked.

Warning: Bosses can fall into this game as easily as employees. A top manager who is playing HANGING ON can be cured by following the steps outlined in the previous game, BUT AT LEAST.

## Beating the game's dilemma

The player deeply involved in this game spent a childhood literally on the horns of a dilemma. On one side, he was told to be compliant and security minded. He was warned of the ravages of economic depression and the bleak days faced by those who gamble and lose. On the other side, he was encouraged to be upwardly mobile and achieving.

Here then are the conflicting drives--one for safety and the other for success. Often, success can't be achieved without risk-taking, so that the player compromises. He goes as far in the business as he can without putting his job on the line, then he settles down to spin his web of tales about what he will some day accomplish.

If the player seems content in a dead-end job and isn't contaminating

194

others with his pessimistic views, leave him alone. In a sense, it's sound practice to allow these players to do their jobs without disturbance. After all, most perform valuable functions without which the business would halt.

# Chapter 27

# GOOD OLD SAM

After years of BUT AT LEAST, then HANGING ON, the unregenerate player may lapse into the role of GOOD OLD SAM. This role is that of an older, honored, knowledgeable person who has gone as far as he can in the business --and has become unpromotable.

Each Sam has a unique story. At one point in his career, everyone will tell you, he was a shining light, a bright guy with a glowing future. But somewhere along the line--nobody knows quite how--he fell into concrete and hardened inexorably into his current position. But he is far from a non-entity: indeed, as soon as he was defined as unpromotable, he became a company institution: Good Old Sam.

Sam has abandoned any thought of taking chances. He values the security of his job over the effort and risks required to break out of his mold.

## A Sam's protective coloration

The look of a Sam is summed up in one word--dowdy. He has blended into his position with such aptitude that he seems part of the furnishings.

When asked about the company's procedures and problems, however, his answers are startlingly clear and perceptive. In fact, one way to diagnose a Sam is to talk to him about the business. As he relaxes, he will crisply define the problems, how they were created, and why they persist. Asked why he hasn't acted to remedy matters, Sam will answer with a shrug that mirrors his feeling that problems come and go, but he'll roll on forever.

## The penalties of discounting a Sam

A common mistake, in these circumstances, is ignoring the wisdom of Good Old Sam--unpromotable employees tend to be discounted. But Sams have much to offer. Example: A company is in the process of being computerized, and forgets to consult the long-service bookkeeper--he's a Good Old Sam. The bookkeeper watches mutely while the accounting system is computerized with several fatal errors built into the system. Of course, the bookkeeper knows where every number is, why it's there, and every other peculiarity of the current accounting system. He grasps how it all hangs together while the people doing the computerization have, besides their computer skills, only general business principles to guide them.

The system is organic; it evolved through years of operation and every working part is stored in the experience of the bookkeeper. But old Sam is willing enough to be ignored. Unprotesting, he watches the computer technicians cut up a viable system and try to stitch it back together, and emerge with a Frankenstein monster.

## Sam in a time of troubles

In times of crisis, a Sam may be promoted to a position of authority:
chances are he will soon become a basket case. His system is no longer
geared to crisis pressures. He gets sick, either physically or emotionally
or both; like an out-of-shape middle-aged man told to run up 20 flights of
stairs, he collapses long before the goal is reached.

## The workings of the lifelong game

And the game need not be a permanent aberration. If Sam wakes up after
his long slumber, don't ignore him for advancement. Sams have been known to
regain their former luster even after top management has long since given
up on them. But some players want nothing more than to be Gold Old Sams all
their working lives--the junior mail boy who at 21 wants nothing more than
to be a senior mail boy when he's 65.

Hard-core players are usually people who had isolated, frightening,
restricted, unsocialized kinds of lives. They were kids locked in closets
by their parents and kept from playing with other kids. Fearful throughout
childhood, with an inability to get along with their peers, the players at
adolescence were five to 10 years retarded in their social development.
They reached young adulthood totally unprepared for it and never caught
up. Usually they are as retarded in social development--relations with the
opposite sex, friendships, and ability to mix in the community--as they
are in the business organization.

## Plugging Sam in

A prevailing irony in today's corporate world is the inclination of

198

top management to hire high-priced business consultants to solve problems that Sam can lick for nothing. In fact, one of the tricks of a business consultant is to ferret out the local Sam, take him to lunch, and pump him for company information. Good Old Sam seldom fails to deliver solid background, reliable facts, and profitable insights.

A Sam can also excel at temporary projects that require a thorough background, such as annual or special reports.

## Serving a vital function

Many work roles filled by Good Old Sams are those no one else would take. Also, there is a minimal necessary number of Sams in every organization--who couldn't be easily replaced. It's a mistake to fire them--it's like knocking down the columns in a Gothic cathedral. Don't be surprised if the roof caves in, no matter how magnificent and soaring the spires.

# Chapter Twenty-Eight

# BITTER— BUT LOYAL

Jack loved his work. Under the tutelage of the head of the company, he was given greater and greater responsibilities. Jack rose to the challenge of the jobs assigned to him with vigor and the boss responded with praise, money, and even more interesting assignments. Because of the boss, Jack enhanced his own self-esteem. Without quite realizing it, Jack began to regard the corporate boss--the man who had done so much for him--as a kind of a god.

Then the boss did something inexplicable. He fired Jack's department head, in what seemed to Jack a particularly heartless manner. Jack was caught in a dilemma. He liked his superior but retained an overwhelming sense of gratitude and affection for the boss. But to stay loyal to the top man meant admitting that the fired department head had deserved what he had gotten. And Jack didn't believe he had.

## A fall from grace

In Jack's eyes, the boss fell from grace. Jack figured that if his superior could be fired so ruthlessly, he might well be next. Jack withdrew into himself as he grew defensive and difficult to deal with. This change in attitude made the boss wonder about Jack; why was he acting so strangely? The boss became critical of Jack, which confirmed to him that his former god was dangerous and not to be trusted. Jack believed he might be fired at any moment.

For Jack, the god-boss was transformed into a devil. Jack even spoke of him as a monster. This talk reached the boss' ears and he got mad, which made him feel and act devilish, just as Jack saw him.

Eventually, the escalating mutual irritation and dislike resulted in incidents that made both Jack and the boss furious at each other. Finally, Jack was fired.

All during this conflict, Jack maintained the facade of being loyal; but he was playing BITTER BUT LOYAL.

## Roots in immaturity

Like many others, the game proceeds out of immaturity. Many employees, including managerial people, hope to find in their superiors an ideal parent who sets an example for vigorous competitive ambition, practices fair play, displays great love of humanity, and lacks all vices--except for lovable quirks. Such a combination of attributes does not exist, but those who wish to believe in it can't tolerate any sign of human frailty in their gods; when events force them to see reality, their resentment and bitterness are all the stronger.

At the job interview, the player is likely to express his awe at the history or reputation of the firm and his attraction to the personal magnetism of the boss. He is obviously seeking employment in hopes that the luster of the place--and its head--will rub off on him.

Usually, the applicant is competent, as well as enthusiastic. A check of the records will probably show, however, that he may have begun work in previous jobs with high enthusiasm, only to tail off and move on--after some unexplained incident.

If you ask the employee why he left the last job, the answer may be "for personal reasons." Less often, the applicant will say something revealing: "My boss seemed to be one kind of man but he really wasn't."

## Advent of bitterness

At first, the player has nothing but praise for the boss-god.

But after a transformation like the one triggered by Jack's experience with the firing of his department head, the player will begin to spill out his bitterness. This early rancor is more or less constrained as the player continues his increasingly transparent pretense of being a loyal employee. He might say of the boss, "He's a good businessman," then add, "But he's really a bastard."

## Piling up of costs

In the early, loyal stage there is no cost as the player overworks in the hope of future rewards and protection from the boss-god. The costs begin during the later, disillusioned stage:

- The player's effectiveness diminishes sharply, especially if his

202

job requires close cooperation with the fallen boss-god.

• New employees' morale may drop in reaction to the player's negative talk about the boss--and the company.

## Effectiveness depends on inspiration—and timing

When the players are inspired by the boss-god, their energy and willingness to learn make them good for any job within their competence--they often fill positions beyond their previously supposed capacities.

Even during the bittersweet stage after the disillusionment, they may continue to function acceptably. Left alone, they can do an adequate job if their bitterness isn't too great. Typically, however, the bitterness slowly becomes a major preoccupation of such employees; their loss of morale and productivity inexorably outweighs their competence. In time, they may be unable to perform any job satisfactorily.

## Relationships with people

When the player is in the loyal stage, he'll mesh with anybody as he makes a big effort that is part of his general enthusiasm for the job. Once he turns secretly angry, he will only get along with very controlled, productive people who neither reinforce the anger nor babble too much about how wonderful the boss and the organization are.

## Step in early

• If you see a player becoming disillusioned, intervene personally. Get the person in for a face-to-face talk, and encourage the ventilation of grievances.

• Confrontation often leads to a positive resolution, which results in a more real relationship between you and the player. If the difficulties cannot be resolved, however, then separation becomes easier, since in effect the player will be in agreement. This averts the agonizing period when the player is secretly bitter but pretending to be loyal.

## Encourage confrontation

Encourage the entire firm to be realistic about everyone's responsibilities and capabilities, including the gifts of the superstars who are the most charismatic managers or bosses. In a realistic and production-oriented environment, employees can confront the boss and discuss how they feel--even about his leadership capabilities.

## Keeping yourself human

You only participate in this game when you accept the mantle of boss-god. Discard that mantle and replace it with one that represents effective, productive leadership without mystery or worship. Here are some ways to make a player appreciate you without transforming you into a god:

• Reveal the operation of your business, strategies and all, as openly as possible. Demystify decision-making and management functions.

• Confess to mistakes and errors in judgment, to confusion and negative feelings; talk about the times when you acted from fear rather than reason. Make yourself human, direct, accessible, and real.

## Limiting hero worship

To a manager some degree of hero worship among employees is often welcome because it makes the acceptance of difficult orders and assignments more palatable. In mild doses, it can be a lubricant that increases productivity.

Also in its mild forms, hero worship can enhance the self-confidence and self-esteem of the boss as he faces the challenges of heading an entrepreneurial enterprise. If this hero worship is maintained in its lowest key, it carries few dangers. Like flirtation, it is even good fun when kept within bounds. It grows disruptive only as its degree of intensity increases.

Chapter Twenty-Nine

# COVER YOUR TRACKS

A player of this familiar game devotes much of his working life to making sure he never takes the rap--whether he did it or not. He assumes that everything that can go wrong will--and that someone else must shoulder the blame. His preoccupation is in keeping the onus from landing on him.

The player doesn't care what it costs as long as he appears blame-free; his driving goal is personal survival. (Since the player is engaged in a rearguard action, he is unlike someone who is "looking out for Number One"; such people seek positive personal advantage.)

## Guarded and defensive

Not every player who comes looking for work brings his game with him. Many players begin their covering procedures only at times of crisis. When things start to unravel and they see colleagues searching for scapegoats, they may get scared enough to start the game out of self-defense.

However, there are some signs that a dedicated player will manifest during a job interview:

• The suspected player expresses an unusual interest in who supervises whom and who can get whom into trouble. Already he is showing the negative, pessimistic, survival elements of the game; he presumes things will go wrong and he wants to know in advance who will be accusing him. In this way, the player reveals his relationship to the paranoid (page 93). Paranoia, however, is an offensive game--strike before you get struck; COVER YOUR TRACKS is essentially guarded and defensive.

• If the applicant has a long job history, he may leave a curious trail among the companies he worked for; that is, a record of corporate failure and trouble. Yet in spite of this pattern, the player maintains that he contributed nothing to these difficulties and assures you he has the documentation to prove it. Yet the fact remains that the player worked for five companies, three of which went bankrupt just before, or just after, he left. Even if the player is blameless, his insistence that you read his files--some of which are 10 years old and deal with companies long since out of business--is a good sign that he's a real player.

## Position papers

One managerial joke has it that the quickest way to root out a player in your company is to do a file/weight analysis: weigh the memo files of everyone at a certain management level; the person with the most poundage for his level of responsibility is presumed guilty of being a player until proven innocent.

The truth behind this assumption is no joke--a practicing player writes memos by the volume. Of course, he saves copies of what he writes and keeps the responses of others, all of which are supposed to establish his blameless position. He is always prepared in case of attack.

He is the guy who makes multiple copies of every scrap of paper worthy of being in the record and then stores them in different places. He may have a complete set of office files at home in case there's a fire in the office or someone steals his copies at work. Usually, this man has a locked file cabinet in his office with one key that he guards jealously.

The endless writings of this player set forth stances in minute detail. He will even stretch the truth a bit when he states in a memo, "As I have warned in the past..." (when there were no such warnings). Among most executives, memos have a way of being thrown away; it's difficult to dig them out to ascertain who said what about whom on what date. Therefore, it's often the player's word--and documentation--against those who are more open and casual in their day-to-day positions.

## An expectation of failure

In conversation the player gives himself away by his questions, which betray his cautious nature: "Who's in on this operation? What do they really want? Exactly how can we avoid trouble? What will our supervisors think if we try this and it doesn't work as planned?" All these queries show that the player expects failure--and the apportionment of blame. (By contrast, the employee who is not playing this game will say things like, "What's the job and how can we get it done?")

When the player is asked a question, he tends to respond as though being grilled by an investigative officer. He'll say things like, "I tried to warn them, but they wouldn't listen."

Example: A salesman realizes that a product made by his company is defective--it has an excessive failure rate. He starts writing memos that indicate his concern about the product. He words his memos carefully so that he is absolved from the product's defects, but he never takes the risk of confronting top management and saying, "We've got to stop sending that junky product out our front door."

## Low risk—high cost

He makes sure that when the ax falls, the production people will feel its blade, not him. His memos prove his awareness--and his innocence. Yet the product remains shoddy, and the company will pay for it.

Other drains on the company exacted by the game:

• The time and effort required to produce the documentation and justification for all his actions deprives the company of the player's productive service. Often the game occupies so much time that the player and his department are immobilized. Work grinds to a halt as workers spend nonproductive hours backchecking every detail of an assignment to be certain the department and its manager-player are spotless.

• As immobilization grips the department, creativity is stifled. Now there develops a rule of fear--employees are afraid to take chances or do anything different that might show up on the record.

• A dedicated player not only affects his department; his contamination also spreads to those he deals with. As his colleagues watch him document his moves and cover his tracks, they begin to take defensive measures themselves. Department after department shows an increase in memo-writing and unnecessary meetings to establish publicly held positions. With everyone braced primarily against political attack, the main purpose of the enterprise--seeing to business--becomes a casualty.

## Some positive roles

One who plays a mild version of this game can be extremely valuable in dealing with government investigative agencies such as the IRS or the Occupational Safety and Health Administration. The player's pessimistic, precautionary posture is quite appropriate in situations involving a true investigator looking for opportunities to cite your business for violation of regulations.

Warning: Be sure the player's attitude is precisely defined as that of an advocate of caution and conservatism. Make it clear that his role is advisory; he doesn't have the final say. His fear can immobilize a corporation. However, his built-in suspicions and abilities for covering up can serve the company when it is being investigated during routine checkups.

Within the corporate structure, a player who adopts the role of conservative devil's advocate can be helpful in decision-making. Sometimes, he is the only one to see trouble spots in a project. Too often, associates shout down the player who objects to every innovation and foresees nothing but problems in every fresh enterprise. As long as he is not taken too seriously, however, this devil's advocate should be given a respectable role in company planning. Not all his doubts will be fanciful.

At a lower level, a player is ideal for a job like quality control manager. It's in his nature to double and triple check.

210

## Proof against paranoia

Players have one dubious distinction: they are among the few who can survive the depredations of a paranoid. The reason lies in the game; since the players are always covering their tracks, the paranoid can never launch a surprise attack.

Naturally suspicious, these players really hit it off only with those who don't threaten them. Since they aren't the glad-handing type, they get along best with other complainers. In general, they tend to be compatible with other pessimists, except those with whom there is a direct competitive antagonism.

If they are placed in jobs where covering is tolerated, they can get along with almost anybody. Secure in the knowledge that his tracks are covered, the player relaxes and becomes friendly.

## Seekers of scapegoats

Optimists have little to share with these players. Likewise, players can destroy naive, trusting people by using them as scapegoats. While the players are documenting their excuses, they shift the blame--often without conscious intention--onto those who have not been covering themselves.

Players tend to abuse those they feel will not strike back. This can be dangerous when the player feels that he can get away with any personal attack so long as he is covered, and can often lead male players to indulge in SEXUAL HARASSMENT (page 41). A male manager, for example, need only write a memo stating that some women are attired too suggestively for work. Then he can attempt a seduction of one of these women, and, if rebuffed and reported, point to the memo as proof that the woman was leading her male colleagues on.

## A matter for self-examination

Managers can find themselves playing this game out of necessity. Example: A chief executive officer is caught between a founding-father chairman of the board and the founder's son, who is being groomed for the top job. As is often the case, the son has little of the father's talent or drive, but the CEO can't tell that to the chairman. If the son doesn't do well, the chairman blames the CEO for not bringing him along properly. The CEO finds himself assuming a defensive survival posture as he is ground between the desires of his boss and the incapacity of the son.

What can a boss, like the CEO, do to end his game--short of quitting his good job? Answer: turn his defensive strategy into a positive stand through honest appraisal. The CEO in our example sat down with the founding father and told him the bitter truth about the son, even though doing so put the CEO's job on the line. As the CEO put it, in spite of all his training efforts, the son was not equipped to handle the top spot. The CEO reminded the older man that it was always possible to fire him--the CEO--and use him as a scapegoat. But the next CEO was going to face the same problem. The CEO's suggested alternative: find a way for the son to reap benefits from the corporation--without running it.

Sometimes, an entire company can play COVER YOUR TRACKS. Example: A conglomerate buys out an independent firm, then through constant interference drives the smaller company's management into a negative, defensive posture. To rid themselves of the game, the abused management must send a message to the conglomerate's board: "You own us and if you want us to quit, you can force us to, or even fire us. But if you continue to interfere and misguide us, our company will go down the tubes, even with managers who do exactly as you direct. Your way of doing things may work for your other companies, but it's destroying ours. In fact, it's forcing us to worry more about covering our flanks than producing a saleable product."

## The skills of pessimistic survival

As practiced in its most extensive form, this game is played by people who grew up with disciplinarian parents who basically believed that if children (or any humans) are unsupervised they will naturally behave wrongly. Another way of expressing that thought: people are basically evil unless kept in line.

The third-degree player learned the skills of pessimistic survival by getting his siblings in trouble while setting himself up as the good guy who ends up being rewarded. The hard-core player also becomes skilled at playing one parent against the other. Dividing and conquering, the player makes sure that none of the evidence points to him as instigator.

With his controlled, accusatory parents, the player learns that it's dangerous to trust indiscriminately--because you're vulnerable, the reasoning goes, you have to learn to look out for yourself. (A paranoid player learns to strike out against the world because he had abusive parents; in this case, controlling parents teach the COVER YOUR TRACKS player to protect himself for survival.)

For example, the parents of a hard-core player could be religious fanatics whose rigid code of ethics makes them inflexible in the raising of their children. They don't grasp the concept that children pass through stages, and they require their offspring to be little adults at all times. To keep their parents from getting angry over their "childish" mistakes, the kids learn to cover their tracks at an early age.

In another setting, a family emerging from a disadvantaged ethnic or racial background into the middle class may be uncertain about its newly acquired status. In trying to eliminate any embarrassing sign of their background, the parents are too strict with their children and hold them to an exaggerated ideal of proper behavior. This approach borders on torture, as the parents exercise unrealistic controls on the kids. On their side, fear of rousing their parents' anger encourages the children to admit to no failings and, if cornered, to shift the blame onto someone else.

Such players are prime candidates for extended group therapy; many of their most negative characteristics would be unveiled in group sessions—the jealousy, the defensiveness, the unwillingness to be vulnerable, the attempts to prove everyone else is wrong.

But even therapy may be difficult. Players intent on covering their tracks in order to prove they have done nothing wrong are capable of mis-hearing, misseeing, and misrepresenting almost anything that casts doubt on them. They convince themselves that they are pure and distrust or ignore any tangible evidence to the contrary.

Chapter Thirty

# YOU'RE HOLDING
# ME BACK

The salesman is ambitious--he wants to become sales manager. The boss tells him that he will be considered for the job if he can attract a wider range of clients. The boss wants not only more sales, but customers in more diverse areas. The salesman hangs back. He fears branching out into new markets. He keeps hoping his superiors will direct the new clients toward him. But his boss, understandably, expects the salesman to show his mettle by digging out the work himself.

Later, the salesman asks for the sales manager's job and is rejected flatly. He is told by the boss that he didn't produce enough of the right kinds of new customers. The salesman blames the boss for not sending that work his way. He says he won't even try to develop new markets if the boss won't support him. In this way, the salesman justifies not doing what he was supposed to be doing. He takes to grumbling about the boss while unconsciously hoping for his help. This condition continues until the salesman either quits or is fired.

The salesman is playing YOU'RE HOLDING ME BACK. Scared to push himself forward and fearing responsibility, the Held-Backer shifts the blame for his inertia and passivity onto a superior whom he actually provokes into holding him back. The provocation varies depending on the personalities. But it tends to signal to the boss that his employee isn't ready for promotion or added responsibility.

Players usually congregate at work to gripe about the men in charge who are holding them back. Rather than gaining the training and experience to enable them to advance, they prefer to moan about lack of support from their superiors. This takes the onus from them and places it on their bosses.

## Attractive hiring prospects

A revealing sign of a Held-Backer is a self-estimate not justified by his track record. His explanation for the discrepancy: others have always held him back--a rationale that is sometimes stated baldly, sometimes subtly. Usually, he will couch it positively: his boss held him back by not supporting him or by not providing adequate personnel, resources, funding, information, training, or something. It is for these reasons he's seeking employment elsewhere.

These players are attractive hiring prospects because they have such apparent potential, though it is less than they are actually willing to exploit. They are often highly anxious before a job interview and they may even throw up in the bathroom under the pressure. Such behavior is an indi-

216

cation that when exciting opportunities arise in the company, the players may choose to be anxious rather than eager. Thus they may seek to avoid the opportunity as they shy away from anxiety rather than capitalize on it to energize them for the challenge.

## A need for support

For the employer as well as for themselves, these players present a difficult problem. Their desire for self-esteem requires them to take on challenging, rewarding positions while scorning routine jobs. Yet they are highly proficient at such routine jobs and prove unreliable when challenged.

Once within the company fold, players tend to dislike situations that arouse the anxiety they survived when they got the job. This means players will perform well in routine functions where they receive lots of support from others. But the player shows signs of severe anxiety when thrust into a novel situation or when confronted by potentially hostile people or a meeting with an angry supplier or customer. Heavy attacks of anxiety may drive the player to manufacture means of avoiding the business--become ill or arrange for a substitute to take his place. If unable to dodge the issue, he may take tranquilizers to allay his anxiety so that he can function at least superficially.

If he handles the feared crisis well, he becomes avid for compliments and other forms of support. This means that you or someone else in authority must spend valuable time before a meeting bucking up the player and mopping his brow. Afterward, you must bestow approval and support with smiles, congratulations, and pats on the back. If the player doesn't receive these attentions, he feels rejected and even more fearful. When the player starts actually ducking out of meetings so that he can bypass his anxiety, he has begun the process of being held back.

## Not suited to new ventures

These players are dangerous in unsupervised, isolated, high-stress, crucial positions. If your firm is entering the export market and you need someone to explore opportunities in several foreign countries, the player of this game is not your choice--no matter how good he is in a domestic environment. He is not suited to work alone with difficult people in another culture.

Difficult people in his own culture are scarcely easier for the player. He won't do well with Takers, particularly nongracious Takers (page 34). He fails with any of the scary people described in this book--Crocodiles, paranoids, and other conmen--who are very threatening to him. Because the player won't be or feel tough enough to deal with such predators, they know they can victimize him.

## An atmosphere of concern, support, and respect

Supervisors should create an atmosphere of concern and mutual respect in which the player helps to realize and develop his own worth. A supervisor must be particularly sensitive to women who play this game. A female buyer with this pattern, for example, functions to best advantage with a strong, supportive supervisor--male or female. Her superior should be willing to accompany her to confront a difficult account or on prickly buying trips. The supervisor must not insist that the player undertake these missions on her own. Such insistence could produce a counterproductive level of stress in the player.

Held-Backers are usually fearful children who were rewarded for timidity by overanxious parents. As adolescents they were punished for being adventuresome or creative. The combination of reinforcement for fearfulness and punishment for risk-taking induces low self-esteem and an unwillingness to take chances.

Since the individuals were encouraged to achieve, at least in a routine way, they are achievement-oriented--hampered by their insecurity and consequently in great need of support from parents, teachers, and other grownups. If this support is not forthcoming, the person learns to use its absence as an excuse to blame authority figures for his failures to take risks.

## Overcoming the past

The boss and other managers can help the player by assuring him that it's all right to take risks. This helps the player overcome the childhood bias imparted to him by his parents.

If the support is offered and the player still won't take any risks, the worker is probably unemployable. Instead of responding to verbal support, the player blames his bosses, the world, God, and the Universe for his passivity, fear, and unwillingness to venture forth to attempt anything. The only solution at this stage is psychotherapy.

Many of these players are charming, skillful, good-hearted people who perform a vast variety of corporate functions well. Since many supervisors and fellow workers are supportive, the players can build self-confidence through continued achievement. One of the positive factors of this game is that it is sequential. That is, as a person matures and ages, a growing record of minor triumphs will increase self-confidence and overcome the historic lack of self-esteem.

Such a player can end up feeling very good about himself; and as fears decrease and securities increase, he can become more and more productive. As a worker, he will never be a great entrepreneur, but he could mature into a solid, competent manager.

# Chapter Thirty-One

# OVERLOAD

OVERLOAD is a bottleneck game. To cover up his inability to handle responsibility, the player allows work to pile up, thus overloading his capabilities. For many managers, the situation furnishes a perfect excuse for their own inefficiency.

Example: A purchasing agent is probably playing OVERLOAD when sales requests aren't being cleared expeditiously. Moreover, incorrect purchase orders are being dispatched and the materials sent reach the work area in disarray--the wrong orders at the wrong places--or in unusable form.

The purchasing agent is definitely a player if these things happen: You can never reach him on the phone (he's always talking to someone explaining the foul-ups). He's always in a hurry, running around, talking, soothing and assuaging. By falling behind, he has to waste many hours a day justifying his behavior.

The player creates and then becomes a victim of his game, which forms a vicious negative cycle. As he falls further behind, he spends more and more of his efforts making excuses. This puts him even further behind, which means he must spend more waking hours in self-justification. Once the player starts circling tighter and tighter while running faster and faster, very little productive work is accomplished.

## The paradox of high personal standards

Most players are highly optimistic and self-confident, and some are even idealistic about what they want from their jobs.

Very often the players who are the best workers will actually fall deeper into the game through their demands on themselves--to accomplish their work at a higher level of performance. They are constantly badgering themselves to get things done faster and better. Yet because the player overextends himself, the work is never completed properly.

The classic delusion of such a player is that he can always perform at his highest and best level, no matter what the conditions. Since no one is always at top form, the player, who has anticipated peak performance from himself, finds that he relentlessly falls behind his overly optimistic schedule, especially during those periods when he is at the lower end of his cycle of competence.

## A crowded life

Players move too fast. They run rather than walk, trot rather than amble. They may have more than one telephone. If you see a manager trying to talk on the phone while going over things with someone in his office and in between shouting instructions to a person in the hallway, you've got a player.

In the terminal stage, the player still wants to maintain his image as fast, smart, and capable. He starts to blame others for overloading him, shifting the responsibility for lack of performance onto the demands made by others.

## Hard work for less than no results

This game carries with it a double loss: the player is intelligent and competent; by allowing him to overload, the firm transforms him into an incompetent bottleneck. Thus the company loses a good worker and inherits a costly problem.

Players tend to become chronic because they're convinced they can handle any problem, even when they're snowed under. Thus they tend to delay diagnosing the problem and continue making excuses to get people off their backs. This attitude causes the player's department to fall behind, which runs up the costs of doing business.

The player of OVERLOAD can keep the game going for a longer time than seems plausible. He does this by convincing his boss that he's just about to make the breakthrough that will solve all their problems. The player is skilled at conveying this illusion, and top managers tend to believe him. After all, the player works like a dog, puts in long hours, and has always been a dedicated employee--if anyone can clean up this mess, he can. Most of the player's accomplishments, however, happened before he started OVER-LOAD.

Obviously, nothing innovative can be done in a department headed by the player. He has all he can do to handle the oldest business in the shop.

To stop the game, the player must be carefully managed so that he is forced to stick to well-defined goals: give him three objectives instead of one and his problem surfaces as he tries to do all of them as fast as possible and succeeds in doing none well.

Any job that can be focused into directing the player's energies toward a single goal without distractions will generally be handled well by the player. Usually, these jobs require heavy doses of direct supervision --monitors to make sure that player isn't taking on too much.

## Removing the load

Some solutions to this game are listed below, the best of which are preventive:

Place those employees who hold overoptimistic expectations in jobs where their attitude isn't dangerous, such as in sales, with its sequential goals (sell A, sell B, sell C). As an alternative, put them under careful supervision so that you are assured their goals are in line with their capacity to perform.

Each task must be objective-oriented, with procedures carefully spelled out. The advance planning should be so thorough that expected problems and routine delays don't precipitate an emergency.

## Fixit steps

If the game is already in progress, try these fixit steps:

Start immediately questioning a suspected player's claims of what he can deliver. Be certain, at the very least, that he has his priorities in the proper order, i.e., that he isn't wasting time on details when he could be at work on the main job.

To give him a chance to do the work--and to deny him an easy excuse for delaying--supply him with adequate resources for the job. Finally, hold him to a strict timetable to clear up the mess he's made with his procrastinating.

## A classic top manager's game

Very often, ranking managers hold onto more responsibility than they can handle. Because they enjoy being involved in all phases of the operation, they can't--or refuse to--delegate authority. As their game causes things to start piling up, they indulge in the player's familiar lament-- they are too busy to accomplish anything.

Bosses who play this game must have colleagues--or a consultant-- confront them about their expansive statements as to what they can achieve. The boss must learn to trust his employees by delegating more responsibility to them. He should limit himself to those areas of work that he does best. He has to keep his hands off those divisions of the company that he would like to run but lacks the time and expertise.

## Overcompensation for early responsibilities

A player in the grip of this game is conspicuous by his harried looks and his constant stream of excuses. His specialty is stating problems in such a way that admits they are insoluble: "We've already tried that and it doesn't work." His voice whines and he never looks you in the eye.

At root, a hard-core player feels so inadequate that he hyperovercompensates by projecting the image that he can do anything--he is Superman. He doesn't slide into OVERLOAD, he dives in head-first.

As children, OVERLOAD players often had a same-sex parent who died, or left the family, or became incapacitated. The player assumed the adult role of that sex long before he was mature enough to do so. In his own eyes, however, he succeeded in acting adult. He grew up nurturing a belief that nothing was so complex he couldn't handle it. Yet he also felt frightened because of the loss of the parent, which left him with deep anxieties.

In its third-degree form, this state is an indication of a severe unrealistic personality disorder that demands intense psychotherapy.

## Positive side of the game

These optimistic people can, with proper placement and supervision, perform at very high levels in the early phases of the game. They will stretch themselves in ways that others can't. There are some built-in problems, however. While the player is performing well, he is planting the seeds that will reap a bitter harvest. He delivers short-term gains while accumulating long-term responsibilities that finally smother his ability to perform.

The point is to keep an eye on a suspected player and initiate solutions before the game consumes him. By keeping the player in his high-performing stage, he is a continuing asset to your company.

PART FIVE

# WORKADAY GAMES

Of the games played in offices and plants, some are less complex than those discussed on the preceeding pages, although to the manager they may appear with annoying and discouraging regularity among his workers. For example, to an employer there are few workers more irritating than one who is always late. Yet the game (CHRONIC LATENESS, page 228) is relatively mild and can be rapidly explored and understood.

Twenty of these first and second degree games are examined on the following pages. Most of them do not stem from deep psychological imbalances; rather, they are behavior patterns with more workaday causes. You will recognize most of them; you may even be playing one or two of them yourself.

# Chapter Thirty-Two

# WORKADAY GAMES

## CHRONIC LATENESS

Some workers are persistently late--late to work, to meetings, in making deadlines, returning phone calls. Basically, these chronically late people are rebellious. They want to determine the routine of their own lives and resent the controls imposed on them by business regulations and their superiors, especially when these strictures are made in the employee's "best interests."

In expressing rebellion, they adopt a passive, indirect method: doing what is demanded, but doing it very slowly. It's not that players don't come to work, they show up late; they don't ignore phone calls, they just take their time calling back. They may be productive employees, but usually complete assignments only after a deadline has passed.

## Investments in rebellion

The players invest a lot of energy in their expressions of rebellion. They spend enormous amounts of time figuring out ways of circumventing systems of control established by the company and the boss. As a result, the usual correctives such as reprimands and confrontations often fail.

Generally, the stricter the enforcement, the more the player disobeys. The supervisor is perceived by the player as unduly controlling; therefore getting even with this authority figure by being late adds spice to the game.


## Meeting the challenge

• Make sure the expectations for the player's work are sensible and can be met with the available time and resources. Set deadlines that can be fulfilled through reasonable effort.

• If the lateness pattern continues, confront the player. Be open and honest in your discussions and convey in no uncertain terms the importance of being on time to the functioning of the company. Negotiate limits that he is willing to commit himself to. Then hold him to them.

• If the player persists in striking out by being late, he is clearly not temperamentally suited for work in a supervised situation. If he is a valued performer, put him on a free-lance basis. Sometimes this loosening of regulations frees the worker and he outdoes his previous performance.

• If he can't or won't work independently and continues flouting timetables, let him go.

Final note: Some players may only cease this game after psychotherapy, which can give them an understanding of their passive-rebellious desire to control their world by telling authority figures what they can do with their rules and regulations.

# PROCRASTINATION

Unlike the CHRONIC LATENESS type who is actually rebellious, the Procrastinator is slow because of anxiety about himself and his work.

In using the telephone, for example, a Procrastinator fears being spoken to harshly or being hung up on. He may be quite capable of addressing someone face-to-face, but will put off using the phone until he has to.

Another fear of the Procrastinator is fear of success. He may complete 90 percent of a job early, then dawdle over the final 10 percent so that the project comes in late. The player's anxiety is that his efforts will not be well received. He delays a harsh moment for as long as possible to avoid the possible pain of criticism or rejection.

A player may also be leery of success on account of the extra effort that will be required of him as a consequence. Once he has done a good job, he will be expected to repeat it. The expectations of his superiors create an intolerable burden on the player and lead him to postpone completion of his projects and thus hold off the judgment day.

## Finding help

Anyone who is this scared and insecure needs professional counseling. A business cannot tolerate a person who is so anxious that he cannot abide hearing his work appraised by his peers and superiors. Often many talented people are gripped by this phobia, however. They are worth the effort it takes to help them to shed their game.

## COMPULSIVE FAST FINISHER

To these people, accomplishing the work ahead of schedule is more important than the quality of the completed product. Their credo: schedules will be met; deadlines take precedence over creativity. This player likes to carry a clipboard and wear a whistle draped around his neck.

Raised in a highly structured household, the player learned early that to get along he had to keep everything in its proper place--disregarding rules meant severe parental disapproval.

To stay within the rules, the young players restricted their creativity and bursts of activity. They ended up with a narrow band of performance that was often thorough but never brilliant.

### Opting for the ordinary

Preoccupied with staying within their circumscribed bounds, the players never try to find an offbeat solution to a difficult problem. In their rush to finish on time, they invariably select the quick, conventional fix. They find it hard to brainstorm or mull over a problem with more creative colleagues. They hear the clock ticking: the deadline approaches. They prefer hack work done on time over inspirational efforts that come in slightly tardy.

### Ruling by schedule

These players usually make difficult managers as they tend to tyrannize every personality type under them through their obsession with punctuality. They are death to creative people who demand time and the sharing of ideas to start their juices flowing.

In certain jobs, however, these players are ideally suited as supervisors. Put them in charge of any task where the methodology is well tried, the problems repetitive, and there is plenty of prickly, detailed work to be gone through. They are perfect for "grind it out" projects where the quality of the project is assured and meeting the demands of the schedule is paramount.

As workers, these players fit right into clerical posts, typing, order taking (but not sales), and production line.

## Helping them bail out

This type of personality regards the seeking of professional help as a sign of weakness. They can only be reached when their anxiety level rises to a height that makes them ill. If they do undertake therapy, however, they latch onto it as tenaciously as they did to their schedules. They follow the routine precisely and, in general, make perfect patients.

## DOUBLE STANDARD

The boss who plays this game usually has much in common with the Procrastinator who fears the very success he is driven to achieve. His craving for success makes him demand that his employees adhere rigidly to the deadlines he imposes. But his fear of rejection leads him to delay honoring his own deadlines.

Here's a common example: The manager of a team project establishes hard-and-fast dates when his colleages must submit their completed sections. He promises that when their work is turned in, he'll pull it all together and arrange a big meeting with top management. The team slaves day and night to finish the project. But after a triumphal presentation to the manager, the work sits on his desk for days and then weeks before he arranges the key gathering of top management.

## The ways out

There are two avenues of escape open to this manager:

1. He can delegate to others the activities that scare him. If he fears making the phone call to summon his superiors, for example--knowing that it makes a meeting with them irreversible--it's a simple matter to have someone else make the call. By the same token, an assistant can attack any portion of the project itself that inspires the manager's fears. Yet, through such skillful delegation, the manager remains in control.

2. A fear of rejection should be worked through by psychotherapy. In this way, the manager can face the tyrant that dwells within him and understand how to deal with it.

## SLAVE DRIVER

By setting deadlines and quotas at the highest achievable rate, the Slave Driver pushes his workers to their maximum every minute of every hour. This manager receives the short-term benefits of high production rates from his driven employees. But he pays a heavy price:

• His employees burn out quickly. No worker, no matter how strong or desperate for a job, can perform flat-out day in and day out. This game only works for the short haul. When the workers are used up, they are discarded like so much machinery and replaced with fresh bodies. The Slave Driver obviously sees workers as disposable resources--and he can draw on lines of hungry people waiting for employment.

• Creative work is nearly impossible under these conditions. Thoughtful workers wither and languish.

## Push for profits

Any manager who deliberately sets out to push his workers until they break, then replaces them, has addicted himself to hyperachievement and profit no matter what the effect on people. Often, he is a Workaholic (page 11).

The deficits of this game are manifold. Skilled people will quit a job under a Slave Driver or learn to give the minimum necessary to get by. For the Slave Driver to maintain his high production quotas, he must become more and more tyrannical as he pushes his workers harder and harder. Eventually, he drives out anyone with any sense of survival and he is left with demoralized peons who are productive only under the lash. Productivity is now lower than it would be under a more sensitive management that takes human feelings and capacities into account.

## Using the game profitably

For businesses that think of people as long-term assets, SLAVE DRIVER is a game that is penny-wise and pound-foolish. It can be turned to advantage, however, when necessary:

1. The Slave Driver can whip up workers for emergencies and short-term bursts of energy. The method must be saved for situations, such as severe business reverses, in which all workers realize the survival of the business is at stake.

2. Be sure that use of Slave Driver is followed by adequate recompense--extra money or time off--so that over the course of a year, workers strike a balance between hyperactivity and compensation.

3. To develop experienced, confident managers in short order, create specialized jobs similar to medical internships. The idea is to have a worker go all out for a clearly defined period of time, not to exceed three years. The stint is grueling, but the payoff is a wealth of solid experience. The worker can tolerate it knowing that its term is limited.

## COMPRESSION FREAK

Highly excitable, this player is intolerant of the ordinary task. The only way he can face it is to make the event dramatic by waiting until the last moments imposed by the deadline. Under this self-imposed pressure, the player turns into a bundle of energy. He now has an excuse for staying up late, having a phone at each ear, and running around as though his office was ablaze. By leaving things until the last minute, he compresses the action required for a task into a short period of time. He uses compression to make his fire burn brighter, just as an internal combustion engine compresses its fuel before firing its cylinders.

## Livening the routine

In business, you pay high prices for this approach:

• Others who aren't playing the game are crushed in the rush.

• You face rapid retaliation from superiors who won't stand for this treatment. Most employers do not relish the anxiety of wondering if the player will complete the job on time.

• A boss who's playing will impose such a strain on his employees that the best will take off and the others will exhaust themselves.

• Since there's no time to consider fine details, meticulous work is impossible.

• If a major error was made in planning, there is no time to make corrections. Contingencies make the COMPRESSION game explosive. A key part that should have been ordered months before is not available when needed. Without the time to search for, or manufacture, a substitute, the project must be finished with whatever is on hand--or fail, or be delayed past the deadline.

• While this breakneck game builds confidence in the addict who can pull it off, it destroys the morale of those who were towed along unwittingly and unwillingly in its wake.

## A simple repair job

Ending this game is simple: break all major projects into a series of jobs, each with a specific deadline. Now the Compression Freak can wait until the last minute to complete each stage without putting the entire effort off until the end. If problems of planning surface, there is enough built-in time to salvage the entire undertaking.

The Freak gets his kicks, the work is done in stages, and the wear-and-tear on his colleagues is reduced to tolerable levels.

236

# PETTY CAPITALISTS

They run numbers and organize football pools during working hours. They sell home products, cosmetics, and magazine subscriptions. They are always hawking one thing or another, using their fellow workers as a natural marketplace for their enterprises. Some even push drugs.

They are the Petty Capitalists, the gamblers and hucksters who are always finding ways to divest your employees of their hard-earned cash. They express their form of petty--and often illegal--entrepreneurship at work because that's where the market is. For many employees, it's convenient to shop while on the job and others like to place bets, play the numbers, or even pick up some pot or hash.

## Putting them out of business

Dealing with the Petty Capitalist is a thorny problem for management. If one player is fired, another will take his place. As long as the market exists, there will be someone enterprising enough to exploit it. The best tactic involves amelioration, prevention, and limitation. Here are some ways to handle the Petty Capitalist:

• Anyone selling narcotics on company time and property should be immediately dismissed.

• Those who purchase drugs at work must be considered candidates for dismissal. Confrontations with the buyers must make it clear that such behavior is grounds for discharge.

• Make gambling forbidden on company property. Break up the betting pools and high-priced card or dice games. Since most employees like to gamble, however, establish some quasi-official operations, such as the World

Series or Super Bowl betting pool. These should be informal and done only with the sanction of management.

• Stop the sale of any products by one worker to another during office hours and in company space. These hucksters waste time, distract workers, and create clear conflicts of interest. There is ample opportunity during off hours for these salesmen to offer their wares to their colleagues.

## Review the sellers

Why are certain people in your employ spending so much time off the job? What is the Petty Capitalist after? The player is usually sociopathic in orientation--by gambling or selling he is ripping off the boss and the system.

The Capitalist uses your plant and time to take advantage of a captive audience. He probably also abuses his privileges with the copying machine and other facilities. Soon he will feel that everything belonging to your company is also his. Once this decision has been reached, theft and embezzlement are not giant steps away.

Knowing all this, review your need for each of these players. Those who are heavily committed to the game should be released.

## JUST BARELY MAKING IT

Driven by anxiety, those who JUST BARELY MAKE IT almost always beat the deadline. But they must torture themselves with apprehension to summon the energy to complete the task. While the Compression Freak likes the feelings he generates by his game, this player is so afraid to finish his

238

work that he must force himself with the negative prod of anxiety.


## Scared Childhood

As a child, this player took heavy criticism at home, particularly about his inability to meet deadlines. He became dependent on his feelings of fear in order to do his work. Just as a parent towering over him scared the player into working, now he relies on the fears generated by anxiety to force him to meet the deadline.

(By contrast, the Compression Freak as a child did only those things that excited him. Indulged by his parents, he often switched his hobbies and interests after the first rush of excitement wore off.)


## Getting by at work

Since everything is put off to the last minute, this game carries the same negative consequences as COMPRESSION FREAK; no time allowed for fresh thinking, reevaluation, unexpected foul-ups, and routine errors. As a result, these anxious players just barely pass muster on the job. They tend to pass the buck, diminish standards, and limit their expectations. These players are so consumed by their fears that they can never be creative.

How to handle them: Break down assignments into stages so that the player's delaying tactics cannot cost the company an entire project--they can be offset in phases. While the anxious player will never attack a job-- late or on time--with the fervor of the Compression Freak, structuring the task will make him more efficient.

The more committed players need consultation or therapy to work through the issues that cause the deep anxiety.

# ABSENT ON MONDAY

One of the most persistent problems facing an employer is worker absences--particularly on Monday. This game is not caused by one psychological condition but many; it is a sure sign that something is wrong.

When a worker signals dissatisfaction by being late or absent on Monday, he is asking for special attention; he may need retraining, reassessment, or reassignment. He may also be requesting disemployment. Unconsciously, he may feel he's in the wrong place or business; by staying out he is saying that he wants you to outplace him, i.e., help him find another position, perhaps in another field.

Nor are the signs limited to Monday absences. The same issues are involved with employees who take extra long lunch hours, leave work too early every day, or regularly slip away well before quitting time on Friday afternoons. In the broadest sense, these are all symptoms of people dissatisfied by that basic company requirement: showing up for work, and staying for the day's full term.

## Drunks, potheads, hypochondriacs

But Monday is in a class by itself: it is the day that everyone has to face it. After a weekend of rest and recreation, Monday morning returns the employee to the hard realities of working life. Difficult tasks must be confronted, awkward situations resolved, reputations once again placed on the line. Most workers accept this challenge by reporting in. But for many different people, Monday morning is not so much a challenge as a sentence. The roll call on Monday may find these players missing:

- Drunks too hungover to respond to the alarm clock.

- Potheads once again out of touch with reality.

- Hypochondriacs who, after a weekend contemplating all their ills, must rush to the doctor first thing Monday morning.

- The depressed people who have collapsed without the work structure. Although returning to work would help them, they have gone into such a tailspin in their free time that they can't answer the bell.

- Showboaters who have overextended themselves to such a point that they cannot return on time--the yacht is still offshore, the hunting party snowbound in the mountains, the flight from the tropics delayed by engine failure.

- Aging jocks who have torn themselves up over the weekend trying to prove that their bodies are still in tiptop condition.

- Romantics who have fallen in love yet again or become so sexually entwined with a mate that they want to continue the ecstasy for one more day.

- Workaholics whose extra jobs--or the punishing schedule at the job you employ them in--has taken its toll.

## A sensitive interview

To discover which of these games the absent employee is playing will require skillful probing in a conversation. The problem may not be one of the forms of weakness or bad judgment cited above, but one that calls for compassion, such as a family illness that keeps the worker traveling long distances over weekends and hampers punctuality at work on Monday mornings. The interview should root out these causes and treat them as fairly and openly as possible. Remember: You, the employer, are the doctor, both literally and figuratively; you are attempting to unearth the disease by discussing the symptoms with the "patient," whose symptom is failing to show up for work.

## Finding the way out

If you discover that the worker has a serious, psychologically based problem for missing Mondays, such as alcoholism or other drug abuse, enlist the proper help.

Should the problem be only that the player would rather be at play rather than work, the time has come for reprimand or censure. Let the absentee know that a high price must be paid for missing Monday--or coming in late and leaving early.

## ODDLY OUT OF UNIFORM

Choice of clothing is a way that all people have of advertising themselves, both consciously and unconsciously. Most employees dress to conform with cultural standards, selecting clothes according to their tastes and personalities while remaining within a range of styles acceptable in a business setting. When the player moves outside the accepted mode of wearing or choosing clothing, the result may be bizarre or distressing--or both. This section briefly examines several different types of nonconformists and what it is that their dress--or their way of wearing clothes--signals about themselves and about their attitudes toward your business.

242

## Slobs

Most Slobs don't like themselves very much--therefore they ignore
what they don't like. This condition is often the result of bad or indif-
ferent treatment by their parents during their childhood. Since their
families put them down, Slobs developed a poor sense of self-esteem, and
they dress accordingly.

In spite of a tendency toward self-deprecation, many Slobs try to win
positive regard through hard work in their jobs. Neglecting themselves
personally, they are highly productive. A shrewd manager can help these
workers break out of the Slob role by judicious counseling. For instance, a
manager can become a father-figure to a player, particularly a young one,
by talking honestly--but with tact--about his dress and comportment. The
employer may even offer to help the Slob select a new wardrobe. Remember,
the player may have lacked good parents; a concerned surrogate father will
most likely be welcomed.

## Rebellious players

Some workers rail against the system by breaking away from every
cultural norm, including the dress code. They wear clothes--such as old
blue jeans in a formal office setting--as if purposely trying to upset
management.

The answer: Try to discover the source of this dissatisfaction. It
may be a phase of self-expression; if the player is otherwise a skilled
worker, try to establish some modest limits to dress. If the player is
rebelling against his work and his clothing interferes with your other
employees or your daily business concerns, let him go.

## Superneat

The standard of acceptable appearance for most employees is neatness, in dress and in work area. Occasionally a worker will needlessly exceed this standard, spending hours of working time in primping and preening, or maintaining a spotless area. This Superneat obsession wastes time and costs your company money. Similarly, managers who force workers to spend valuable time in being overly orderly are misdirecting energies.

The answer: have a Dutch Uncle chat with the worker or supervisor to redefine the boundaries between neatness and Superneatness.

## Flamboyant

It has become common in the business world to see workers, and sometimes managers, indulge themselves in flamboyant dress--formal wear in humble settings, exotic leisure outfits such as velvet jogging suits, decorative printed robes or dashikis, and other ethnic dress.

In contemplating this extravagance, ask yourself a basic question: Is this attire disturbing operations or distracting customers or fellow workers? If the answer is no, then say nothing. If such a mode of expression is a nuisance--the tinkling of dangling jewelry, for example, can serve as an irritant that can slowly drive listeners to a mild frenzy--talk to the offender. Set some reasonable bounds determined by the effect the dress is having on others.

## Oversexy

Today's casual clothes and informal styles are generally widely accepted as long as they are not carried to extremes. Men and women who squeeze themselves into skin-tight outfits and then leave the front buttons or zippers open to the navel are breaking the bounds of decorum. Oversexy dress is guaranteed to distract other employees--nor should those offended have to carry the burden of constantly complaining about it. One word of objection is enough for you as the boss to have a talk with the Oversexy Dresser.

WARNING: The job of the manager is not to force everyone to dress as he does, unless it is traditionally required. Staying within the confines of currently accepted workday styles, however, is not considered an imposition of the manager's will on his underlings.

## Body odor

Some employees who dress within the prescribed bounds still offend unintentionally or otherwise by their body odor. This symptom may be the sign of severe psychological or medical disorder. For example, not bathing or poor hygiene even after pointed hints suggests a disturbed personality. These players are ignoring social modes for their own reasons. In their game they hit such high levels of denying reality that they cannot smell themselves and they deny the reality of their odor. This is a sure sign of a serious problem that demands professional counseling.

The player could have a medical problem he has told no one about. Some diseases have an accompanying odor; diabetes, for instances, causes circulatory problems that could lead to foot sores that do not heal properly, with an accompanying smell.

No matter what the cause, your obligation is to conduct a sensitive interview. This problem is ill served by command, directive, or dictum.

The subject is extremely intimate and highly sensitive; it must be approached in the most civilized manner.

There may be no quick or easy answer to the problem of body odor. But just the simple act of discussing it with the player will sometimes provide the initiative for him to seek help from a medical doctor or a psychotherapist.

## SURLY AND UNCOOPERATIVE

These games are two facets of the same problem. The employee playing SURLY generally is in a position to display his ill temper to the public. Uncooperative plays his role at work with his boss or fellow workers. In both games, the player lets his personal unhappiness manifest itself through a disagreeable attitude.

Surly moans about his miseries with his employer--he is unpaid, he is not appreciated, his benefits are substandard. Miserable in his work, he comes to believe that he would be better off if he did not have to deal with the customers that keep the company alive. He shows this by being antagonistic to those he is paid to serve.

In some cases, a Surly is presented to the world as a result of the organization's own lack of proper training programs and adequate supervision. An unhappy employee who has not been taught how to relate with the public can easily fall into the SURLY game. It is not hard to pinpoint an organization that has a faulty training program, especially a company whose business involves dealing with the public, such as a restaurant, hotel, or store.

## Training is the answer

All workers will have problems, but those who are paid the standard wage and benefit package can be taught to leave their personal difficulties at home.

There are many kinds of training programs available to help disgruntled employees improve their comportment. Indeed, these are among the most highly sold products in the organizational development field--teaching people to relate better with others. Lists and catalogues of these programs are obtainable through such organizations as the American Management Associations, 135 West 50th Street, New York, NY 10020.

Private consultants can also devise special programs for your business needs, most of them based on improving human relationships.


## The uncooperative game

Lack of adequate training also feeds the growth of the UNCOOPERATIVE game. Although its roots are buried deep in the player's personal unhappiness, training can make him a more effective--and more agreeable--worker.

The Uncooperative player is often an assistant or secretary who works in close coordination with the manager. He displays his disdain for his job and his employer by fighting him every inch of the way. Often the boss indulges the player for fear of being disliked.

In this case, both the boss and the Uncooperative worker need help from a consultant. If the player continues to be Uncooperative, he should be let go. With so many willing and pleasant people available in the personnel marketplace, there is no reason why a manager should tolerate an Uncooperative who refuses to reform.

## OFFICE ROMEO/OFFICE TEASE

Both Romeo and Tease share one major trait; they respond to difficult problems at work through sexuality. As business problems depress them, they seek relief through sexual excitement. This may ease the depression temporarily, but it won't solve the troubles at work. Increased problems only lead the players into greater sexual activity, which completes the now familiar vicious cycle of these games.

The Office Romeo lives to display his sexual prowess--sometimes real but usually imagined. He loves to prove to himself and his colleagues that he is skilled at something. He can be a lovable, attractive man who likes to control his environment, but what worries him?

• His father may have been a ladies' man and he is role-modeling.

• He could have been raised in a conservative, hyperreligious, antisex environment and he is rebelling to escape it.

### Over- or undersexed?

The tantalizing question about a blatant Romeo is, "Is he oversexed, or undersexed and overcompensating?" He could be either. If oversexed, he clings to the Romeo role as a game in which he is accomplished. He is proud of his abilities and wants the world to know. By contrast, he might have been an undersexed youth who suddenly realized what he was missing. In reaction, he assumes the role of office lover.

Of course, there are all sorts of players between these two ends of the spectrum--some may even be playing a specialized game that could be called ALL TALK, in which the flirting and promising is more important than the consummation of the sexual act. These players feel sexually inadequate; they want to play the game to restore their faith without the obligation to perform.

## What motivates the Tease?

Almost every male knows the line of the Tease: "Come close. Stop!" The woman who plays the Tease is taking on a complex game. Often she is sexually repressed--mocking the men she turns on. In a basic conflict, she desires to be attractive sexually. Yet really she yearns for men to like her without regard for her sex. The conflict plays itself out as she attracts males through her sexuality--then rejects them. She turns on men only to do to them what she does to herself--repress the sex drive.

## When to intervene

Managers should only interfere with these games when they become grossly obvious. An outsider (the Boss) can seldom comprehend all its intricacies. If a worker is also a friend, a gentle word of warning may be in order. Otherwise, wait until the player is actually beginning to fail at his job before calling him in for an interview. Even then, never forget that the talk must be accomplished with the utmost dignity and awareness.

Special note: It is often awkward for a male manager to discuss this subject with a Tease. He may well fear that she will misinterpret the manager's concern as sexual interest on his part. Men should always have a female office manager present in an interview about sex. When possible,

have the female manager do the interviewing with the Tease. This tends to
remove the obvious misunderstandings.

## SELF-RIGHTEOUS

Filled with anger over the slights or injustices suffered during his
life, a righteously indignant person lies in ambush, waiting for someone
to make a mistake. Once he spots one, this venom-filled worker strikes,
usually in elaborate ways. First, he sets up his victim with praise: "I
really admire the way you're handling your job. I don't know how you keep
composed under all that pressure and strain. But there's one little thing
that's been bothering me..."

Then, whap! The worker unleashes a torrent of verbal aggression triggered by some real or imagined error he perceives in the victim's behavior.
The recall--and imagination--of the player are prodigious and he usually
leaves the victim limp and sweating.

## The making of a player

What type of person harbors such resentments and unleashes them so
passionately? Usually, the player had a righteous parent whose role he is
modeling. Often, his anger is directed at the parent he is imitating: the
parent would often change the rules to put the child-player in the wrong no
matter what he did. Unable to combat these rule shifts, the player realized
early the advantages of being "right." And in attacking those who make
mistakes, he is getting back at the very parent who taught him the SELF-
RIGHTEOUS game.

250

## Make no errors

The only certain way to keep a Self-Righteous player from attacking is to make no mistakes. Since this is impossible, be frank and open with him in your dealings. The best approach is to draw up detailed hard-and-fast contracts setting forth his jobs and responsibilities, while asserting your authority as boss.

Right from the start you must make yourself clear to the player: "We all make mistakes. We all profit from feedback and corrective suggestions, so I want you to tell me when I've made an error. But that's not an invitation to get your kicks by jumping on my miscalculations. Let's treat each other civilly and with respect. Let's not use unintentional errors as an excuse to get mad at the universe--and me."

In dealings with those outside your own sphere of control, the best defense against this game is a nondefensive posture. If you make a mistake and are attacked for it, let the player spend his energies and then say, "You're right. I was wrong." This always bursts what's left of his balloon.

If the attacks persist, try humor. These players can't stand to hear laughter--they have too much hate in them. The point to remember is this: defuse the confrontation as quickly and deftly as you can. The player thrives on the assault--it justifies his anger.

## CHRONIC COMPLAINER

Nothing proves more inviting to a Chronic Complainer than a captive audience--a crowded elevator or a room full of people who cannot leave. Now he has an abundance of victims, people whom he can depress with his miseries, burdens at work, and the slights he suffers.

## Causes for complaints

Some players have been unhappy since they were children when they suffered a series of sad or traumatic events. They spend their adult lives gathering evidence that proves how miserable life can be.

Some lived in families where being happy was dangerous. They had unhappy parents and siblings who would turn on anyone showing signs of enjoying themselves. The players learned to bitch and moan, no matter how they felt inwardly, in order to survive.

A number of players do not develop their game until later life when personal reverses or disappointments have caused severe depression. Remembering only their ill fortune, these players ignore what is positive about their lives and concentrate only on its bleak side.

(Extreme Complainers are saving up for suicide. By brooding only on the world's miseries, they are justifying the terminal relief of death.)

## Dumping their miseries on you

People who are temporarily depressed often feel better after a talk to a friend. The Complainer, however, revels in dumping his load of miseries on you when opportunity arises. He loves to tour the place of business telling his audience of his problems and leaving his listeners feeling worse than he does.

This insistent unburdening enables the Complainer to feel that he is not alone in his plight. It also conveys to him an esteem and power because others are now actually worse off than he is: he has proven again how fragile is happiness. He proclaims loudly that unhappiness is the only reliable element in this tricky, untrustworthy existence. Depression is secure, misery is safe. And everything seems to support this pessimistic view--the news media, the publication of mass market paperbooks on lurid and sensational subjects, horror movies, and TV shows about human depravity. The Chronic Complainer is well armed with evidence of what a rotten place the earth can be. Even on your strongest, most positive days, his insidious attacks are difficult to repel.

## Piercing the veil

To determine whether the player is just a petty griper or a Chronic Complainer, examine his complaints. Solve those problems that you can and see how that affects the player's attitude. If he immediately comes up with fresh complaints, you have a chronic player on your hands.

Chronic Complainers need professional help. Help them receive it, but if their moaning at work continues, rearrange their schedules to deny them as much access to other employees as possible. Let the player tell his problems only to a therapist.

# BABBLING

In this game, the player is afraid not to be seen as taking responsibility. Played by highly ambitious, overanxious risk-takers, the game conveys the sense that the person is full of ideas--he's on top of things. In reality, the player is driven to respond before he knows what he is going to say. The result is torrent of BABBLING, words that buy time for the speaker until he can formulate his thoughts.

Practiced Babblers can string many complex words into complicated sentence structures. While this verbal performance can be amazing, the net effect is to plunge the audience into a stupor.

## Turning off the babble

Babblers were usually the children of highly ambitious parents, trained to grasp things quickly, no matter how difficult. Lacking information, their thoughts unformulated, their impulse is nevertheless to speak out--to prove their awareness.

Dealing with a Babbler in a meeting, the chairman should ask him what his line of argument is--where he is headed. If the player cannot summarize his theme, he should be asked very kindly to hold his response until he clarifies the points he is trying to make. Couch this advice in the most generous terms since the Babbler cannot lose face--you will turn him off and you may lose an imaginative source of ideas.

To help the Babbler divest himself of his game, conduct individual conferences in which he works toward committing himself to restraint. Remind him that his ambitious are best served if he is viewed at meetings as thoughtful rather than impulsive.

## Thinking on your feet

Some players find it impossible to hold an interior dialogue and need to hear their own voices before they know their thoughts. In its best form, this is called thinking on your feet--or out loud. More often, it is a process of talking around a subject until an idea emerges.

In small meetings, this might be permitted, especially if the player seeks permission of the others. The usual question is something like, "Let's just talk idly about this and see what comes out." When everyone is aware and participating, this can be a valuable form of brainstorming.

But the procedure can be disaster at large meetings where many others with ideas already formulated are anxious to be heard. Players under these conditions should keep still or limit themselves to reading prepared statements.

## HUMBLE MUMBLE

Burned often at meetings in the past by negative reactions to his ideas, the Humble Mumbler fears adverse responses. Yet he is convinced that he can contribute to a meeting. To protect himself and avoid responsibility for his statements, he minimizes his ideas through a preamble of self-deprecations. A player precedes any serious statement with a series of disclaimers that sound like this: "I'm not very smart and I certainly don't belong in this learned meeting and I know I wasn't thinking clearly when I came up with this idea, but I have this plan that will waste your time if you consider it but I thought I would ask your indulgence. Would you like to hear it?"

By this time his listeners are paying no attention, so that if he makes an error, they will probably miss it. Also, they may have taken enough pity on the player to withhold any immediate criticism of his idea.

If the idea actually does have merit, the player has several options: (a) he can claim credit for it, which raises his profile and leaves him vulnerable to defending it; (b) he can watch its growth from the back of the room without risking accountability for its future history.

By nature, the Humble Mumbler prefers to be quickly forgotten. His contributions to a meeting are like babies left on the steps of the local convent.

## Paying the price

While the player retains the anonymity he seeks, he abdicates any chance for reward. He may claim that this is what he wants, but he may be lying to himself.

The issue here is one of courage. As a manager, you can encourage the player to stand by his ideas and suggestions through support and by cutting through his Humble Mumble preambles. By advising a player to abandon his disclaimers and state his positions more boldly, you may transform a retiring idea man into a confident manager.

## DISTRACTER

After one or two sentences from this player, his listeners' frustrated groans announce the death of constructive discussion. The Distracter deftly turns the meeting toward minutiae, irrelevant histories, obscure objections, or anything else that commands attention--while impeding progress. A prime offender is a former chairman who spins endless tales of the days when he was in charge--complete with every detail of how he solved all the problems.

Another prominent Distracter is the purveyor of doom, which he sees lurking in every issue. His preference for pessimism is classically self-protective--if he sees the bad, he'll be prepared for its arrival.

These players have a kinship with spectators at sports events who throw bottles at the players or umpires. Like unruly fans, they should be silenced or ejected.

A polite way to put them back on the track is to ask them to repeat the main issues being discussed and to briefly indicate the relevance of their contribution. If they find this impossible, rule them out of order and proceed to the next speaker.

## BLUSTERS (AND YELPS)

Players use loud voices like clubs to subdue the opposition--or anyone trying to offer anything new. They thunder their views, shout down dissent, and ridicule all opposition. Thus do they attempt to take over a meeting that they cannot control through the force of ideas.

A strong chairman must hold a tight rein on these players. He must demand that they simmer down, articulate their position once, and then not comment on the arguments of others except when recognized by the chair, and only in a civil manner.

## BULLY IN THE CHAIR

Nothing can dominate a meeting more destructively--and undermine debate faster--than a chairman who abuses his power to force things to go his way. Relying on the established rules of parliamentary procedure and the inherent authority of the chair, this player short-circuits discussion and pushes through his measures in dictatorial fashion.

The classic ruling of the Bully in the Chair goes like this: "May I hear how many are for a unanimous decision. Any opposed? The majority votes for a unanimous decision. The motion passes unanimously."

A favorite trick of the player is to rule out of order any person who speaks eloquently in opposition to his position.

The only way to combat the Bully in the Chair is to call for an adjournment of the meeting. That will give your forces time to regroup, and try either to have the chairman replaced or to make him return to the rules of fair play.

## PSYCHOLOGICAL HYPOCHRONDRIACS

In search for solutions to psychological problems created by others, some of my readers may have identified themselves with the difficulties at a level more serious than is real for them. If so, they have become Psychological Hypochondriacs, playing a game in which they feel they are suffering from one or more of the conditions described here.

Those who play PSYCHOLOGICAL HYPOCHONDRIAC fall into a repetitive pattern that involves discovering new shapes in which to pour their old feelings of hopelessness, incompetence, frustration, anger, sadness, and the like.

Some care needs to be exercised in dealing with the material in this book. When discussing the games with employees, remember to emphasize that choosing new shapes for old patterns does not change anything. The only thing that works is the selection of new options and fresh attitudes with which to face real problems.

Psychological Hypochrondria is not only a way to take on a lot of the ailments described here, but a means of preventing any real solutions to the problems that do exist. Don't add to your current headaches by encouraging this futile game. Instead, concentrate on making clear the new options open to the player and to you. They will help everyone make the choices that will deliver satisfactory outcomes in your lives.

Available from BOARDROOM® BOOKS:

**The Complete Guide to Running A Business** *by John R. Klug.* 3,989 powerful ideas covering every area of your company's operation. This volume will help you slash costs, increase sales volume and fatten bottom-line profits. Over 300 information packed pages, fully indexed. $50.00

**Business Computers: A Guide to Selecting Hardware, Software and Services** *by Dick H. Brandon & Sidney Segelstein.* Two experts reveal how to select the right computer for your data-processing needs, at the best price, with the least grief. 308 pages. $50.00

**Accounting for Owners and Managers** *by Merwin Leven.* What you need to know about cost accounting and control, lease vs. purchase decisions, cash flow and the basics of keeping books. 140 pages. $50.00.

**Finding Money** *by James G. Hellmuth.* Where the money is—private sources, public sources, financing for every business purpose. $50.00

**The Encyclopedia of Practical Business.** 400 pages of shrewd business know-how compiled by the editors of Boardroom. Covers subjects in business and personal management. 27 chapters; indexed; 732 separate articles. $50.00.

**Squeeze-Outs** *by Bertil Westlin.* How unwanted or unproductive associates are maneuvered into relinquishing interest in closely held corporations and partnerships. $95.00.

**Winning Stock Selection Systems** *by Gerald Appel.* Treasury of modern investment knowledge. 114 ways to improve timing, prevent mistakes, reduce risks, and interpret market signals. Apply powerful stock market indicators to profit in bull & bear markets. $50.00.

**The Book of Business Knowledge** Compendium of business, financial and legal knowledge. Run a company better; master new executive skills. All in plain English by 178 experts on every aspect of business. $50.00.

**Inventory Strategies** *by Norman Kobert.* Inventory reports that set priorities for action. Easy and efficient systems for monitoring inventory. $50.00.

**Managing Time** *by Norman Kobert.* 168 ways to work smarter instead of longer. How to get more done, with less stress, in less time. $50.00

Send check or money order to<br>
Boardroom Books, 500 Fifth Avenue, New York, NY 10110